Transformation Towards Human-Centered Medical Devices
Service Design for Product Management

Ida Koho

Co-author: Antti Brunni

Layout & cover: Xavier De La Huerta

Editing: Lotta Leppälä

Publisher: BoD · Books on Demand, Mannerheimintie 12 B, 00100 Helsinki, bod@bod.fi

Print: Libri Plureos GmbH, Friedensallee 273, 22763 Hampuri, Saksa

ISBN: 978-952-80-9402-9

Preface

Who should read this handbook?

This book was written for busy medical device professionals who seek professional growth and wish to keep their skills up to date. It's a good fit for anyone who likes to learn more about using human-centered approaches along technology-centered ones. The handbook is short and easy to read. **It takes the perspective of product management, but it can be a great resource for a wide range of medical device professionals regardless of their specific roles or backgrounds.** Visitor author Antti Brunni will discuss service design when the medical device is software.

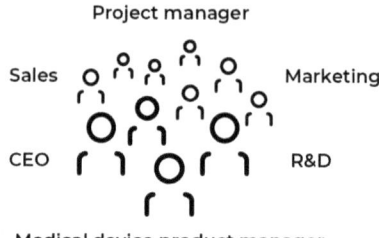

This book is for you if you already see the added value service design brings to medical devices and wish to start applying it in practice. It's also for you if you are unfamiliar with service design but would like to understand the basics and discover the opportunities service design and design thinking have to offer. It's for you if you seek a new approach to liven up your professional life as well as the lives of patients, physicians, nurses, laboratory personnel, or other customer segments.

This book is a valuable resource for those who wish to observe and re-evaluate current working methods. It offers tools for recalibrating practices and increasing user involvement in product development.

As a **product manager or CPO**, you might use the book as an inspiration for all practical duties related to user research and user involvement in product development. Employing service design not only brings you closer to the users but also assists you in communicating with your internal customers. This handbook may also help you articulate the benefits of user involvement and human-centricity when talking to your colleagues.

Service design is a suitable approach whether your organization is a start-up, a scale-up, a small or middle-sized company, or a multinational corporation – public or private. Your product type could be a me-too product, a mass product, or a high-end device with a narrow target group – new or old.

Are you new to product management? Find the description of medical device product management and other key concepts on pages 81–83 and examples of product manager customer personas on pages 57–58.

How to read this book

Read
1

Read and scan the book, focusing on what feels relevant at that moment. There are tips, sources, or keywords on every page. Actively research different topics and talk with AI while reading the book.

Process
2

Let your mind process what you have learned. Analyze and criticize.

Iterate
3

Read the book again with an open mind, using the same active reading style. The amount of time you invest in each topic is your choice.

Search or chat with AI

The text boxes and **bold text** contain keywords or topics that might be useful to research further. You can utilize search engines or AI for inspiration. Remember that content created by AI may contain errors and inaccuracies.

Note #1
This is not a book on product development. Instead, this book addresses a variety of topics related to medical device business and medical device product management, including product development, user involvement in the development process, customer value creation, cost of service design and its implementation, ideation, prototyping, and many other important aspects of successful medical device business.

Note #2
This book does not suggest we should replace the process of medical device product development with the service design process. It aims to inspire the reader to start using the service design process, tools and mindset to increase the human-centricity of medical device products and development processes.

Note #3
Service design is not a cure-all. However, by applying service design, a medical device manufacturer may increase product safety, clinical effectivity, and patient and user satisfaction. It may even reveal new business opportunities.

Summary

- Part I explains the purpose and **background** of this handbook. It also presents the current situation of service design in medical device manufacturing.

- Part II explains **what service design is** from three perspectives: service design as a process, a toolbox, and a mindset. The definition of the service design approach often depends on its user. A person with a background in sustainability and circular economy will likely explain service design differently from someone producing digital or AI-supported services. Still, underneath, the design principles are the same. Part II aims to summarize service design in a way that is easy to understand and apply, even if this is your first time hearing about service design.

- Parts III and IV aim to answer the questions of **for what purposes** a medical device product manager or manufacturer could use service design **and why** they should do so. It offers suggestions on how to start using service design and may help you pitch service design to the director level.

- Part V walks you through the entire **service design process** (discover, define, develop and deliver). Along the way, you'll get tips and examples on how to do service design.

- The last chapter summarizes the handbook and suggests next steps.

After reading this handbook

You will have the basic knowledge to start using the service design approach to invent, innovate, and optimize
You will be able to explore new ways of thinking and working
You will have some practical tools for user involvement and co-creation
You will have a process to brighten up many product management tasks
You will better understand the language service designers speak

About the authors

Ida Koho, Biotechnology Engineer BSc., MBA, has a decade of work experience from medical device manufacturers of different sizes and clinical areas. During her professional journey, Ida has worn many different hats from product management to branding, marketing management, product training, and customer support. She has gained practical service design experience in projects related to energy transfer using blockchain technology, brand strategy, health mobile app, and the creation of this handbook.

"The more I practice service design and learn about it, the more convinced I am about the match between service design and medical device product management. Service design has made me more efficient, confident, and creative in my role as a product manager. It has given me versatile tools and motivation to increase user research and user involvement. If there had been a service design book specifically for medical devices, I would have loved to read it. But because there wasn't one, I started looking into how to create one.

I firmly believe that a human-centered design approach like service design will lighten product management work and increase a positive clinical impact. Those are my biggest motivations to spread the word of service design among medical device manufacturers. This book is my way of celebrating the fact that both you and I can now have our own process for the diverse and constantly evolving work of medical device product management! Isn't it wonderful to trust the process and let it help us in communicating, organizing and creating?

Additionally, a human-centered approach like service design will impact the performance of the entire organization, if adopted in the company culture. I hope this book initiates inspirational discussions and encourages medical device manufacturers to publish service design case studies. By sharing experiences, both successes and failures, we can develop best practices and prove that medical devices and service design truly are a good fit."

Antti Brunni is an experienced expert in service design and digital strategies, with over 15 years of experience in developing and managing digital and data-driven services, particularly in the fields of health and well-being.

Antti has a strong academic background: he holds a Master of Arts degree in Digital Media from the University of Lapland and is currently pursuing doctoral research focused on design strategies for medical software and supporting clinical decision-making. His interdisciplinary expertise bridges technology, design, and healthcare, making him a significant contributor to the research of service design and innovations in medical devices.

As a writer, Antti leverages his extensive professional experience and academic knowledge to provide practical tools for product management and service design professionals to improve the safety, usability, and regulatory compliance of medical software.

Contents

Part I: Introduction

Part II: Outlining Service Design

Part III: Service Design for Medical Device Product Management

Part IV: Service Design for Medical Device Manufacturer

Part V: How to Do Service Design:
Process phases step by step

Discover

Define

Develop

Deliver

Conclusion

Part I

Introduction

Why do we need another book on service design?

"Along with business and technology considerations, innovation should factor in human behavior, needs, and preferences. Human-centered design thinking – especially when it includes research based on direct observation – will capture unexpected insights and produce innovation that more precisely reflects what consumers want."

Tim Brown: Design Thinking
Harvard Business Review 2008

In the above quotation, Tim Brown summarizes the human-centered design approach, the ideology behind service design. Combining this mindset with the framework of (IVD) medical device standards and regulations increases the likelihood that the developed medical devices are safe and clinically relevant as well as meet customer demand and expectations. Standards and regulations stress the importance of focusing on the user but, naturally, do not offer practical tools to achieve this. Medical device products are more than goods. As a practical, human-centered, and holistic approach, service design can complete the medical device manufacturer's toolbox for designing the **aspect of service and experience.** Service design may help close the distance between the product manager and the customer and help co-create added value.

Over recent decades, service design has shown its versatility, serving a range of purposes from organizational strategy to product and service development. The master's thesis research this handbook is based on concluded that service design remains underutilized by medical device and IVD medical device manufacturers and that industry-specific service design content is needed to increase awareness in the industry. Service design has increasingly been adopted by organizations across various industries, including companies involved in emerging technologies. It's time for medical devices to follow suit.

Numerous case studies have highlighted service design's potential to optimize healthcare operations and patient experience in hospitals and other caregiving settings. On the other hand, there is little evidence of medical device manufacturers using service design.

Service design is used

In this book, **the healthcare industry** refers to organizations and services that provide medical care and support in hospitals, other care centers, or at home. It may also refer to clinical research, healthcare technology and healthcare information flows or delivery models.

Medical device manufacturing
- IVD MD
- MD
- Software

Product Management

Service design not common

In the worst case, **medical device manufacturers lack systematic user involvement and needs-driven product development, which leads to innovations that are predominantly product- or technology-driven. A culture of training the user on poorly designed products instead of developing the products to fit the user's cultural context or capabilities has been observed in the medical device industry.** A medical device product manager is often responsible for translating the voice of the customer to the rest of the development team. Co-creation with the medical device user may not be straightforward, but it's often vital or at least worth the effort. This book aims to provide practical resources to improve user involvement in all types of product management projects, including product development.

Based on academic literature, involving the user in product development brings multiple benefits for both the user and the manufacturer. However, literature also suggests manufacturers face challenges with involving the user.

Benefits of user involvement
- increases product safety
- improves the health of patients
- provides access to user experiences and ideas
- improves usability and understanding of the user's cultural context
- improves clinical effectivity
- helps to meet user needs and clear clinical needs
- ensures that the correct device is developed

Challenges of and attitudes towards user involvement
- manufacturers do not always perceive end users (especially patients) as a key success factor
- lack of resources and the perception that human-centered methods are too resource intensive
- may commence a time-consuming ethical approval process
- lack of use and/or understanding of formal user research methods
- product development processes failed to provide the necessary guidance and support for the establishment and enforcement of the use of rich and valid user insights

The service design tools, thinking and process may open new ways to do **product management**. They lighten the product manager's load of communication, administrative, and development tasks. Service design a good approach for strategy, troubleshooting, and (user) research. Like one co-creator of this handbook said:

"It's not a new idea to base product development on the voice of the customer, but it's great to have a process for that."

Service design benefits both external customers and the organization's employees. The advantages of service design become most evident when it's implemented throughout the organization. Medical device product management and related functions can be a viable path to introduce the service design approach in a medical device manufacturing organization.

For organizations, service design may provide
- deep exploration of competitive advantages and market demand
- transition from innovation to creating value for profitability
- attraction and retention of a new generation of talents
- a way to dispel organizational silos.

To conclude, this book aims to inspire the reader to increase user involvement through design thinking and service design. It explains why, where, and how a medical device product manager or manufacturer can use service design.

The handbook's principal mission is to help you take the first steps in service design and get inspired about design thinking in the field of medical devices. Additionally, it provides tips for further reading and may assist you when pitching service design within the organization.

This handbook was co-created with experts of IVD medical device product management, service design, and medical device ISO standards. The next chapter explains how this co-creation happened and how the service design approach was used to design this handbook.

1. Bridgelal Ram M., Grocott P. R., & Weir H. C. (2008). Issues and challenges of involving users in medical device development. Health Expectations, 11(1), 63–71.
2. Bitkina, O. V., Kim, H. K., & Park, J. (2020). Usability and user experience of medical devices: An overview of the current state, analysis methodologies, and future challenges. International journal of industrial ergonomics, 76, 102932.
3. Hamid, U. Z. A., & Suoheimo, M. (2023a). Introductory chapter: Service design for emerging technologies product development. In: Umar Zakir Abdul Hamid, & Mari Suoheimo (eds.). Service Design for Emerging Technologies Product Development: Bridging the Interdisciplinary Knowledge Gap, pp. 3–7. Springer.
4. Juuso, I., & Seppänen, T. (2023). How the service design approach can empower medical device development to reach its user-centered goals. In: Umar Zakir Abdul Hamid, & Mari Suoheimo (eds.). Service Design for Emerging Technologies Product Development: Bridging the Interdisciplinary Knowledge Gap, pp. 101–115. Springer.
5. Martin, J. L., Clark, D. J., Morgan, S. P., Crowe, J. A., & Murphy, E. (2012). A user-centered approach to requirements elicitation in medical device development: A case study from an industry perspective. Applied Ergonomics, 43(1), 184–190.
6. Money, A. G., Barnett, J., Kuljis, J., Craven, M. P., Martin, J. L., & Young, T. (2011). The role of the user within the medical device design and development process: Medical device manufacturers' perspectives. BMC Medical Informatics and Decision Making, 11(1), 15.
7. Rinkus, S., Walji, M., Johnson-Throop, K. A., Malin, J. T., Turley, J. P., Smith, J. W., & Zhang, J. (2005). Human-centered design of a distributed knowledge management system. Journal of Biomedical Informatics, 38(1), 4–17.
8. Shah S. G. S., & Robinson I. (2007). Benefits of and barriers to involving users in medical device technology development and evaluation. International Journal of Technology Assessment in Health Care, 23(1), 131–137.
9. Shah, S. G. S., & Robinson, I. (2008). Medical device technologies: Who is the user? International Journal of Healthcare Technology and Management, 9(2), 181–197.
10. Yang, F., Al Mahmud, A., & Wang, T. (2021). User knowledge factors that hinder the design of new home healthcare devices: Investigating thirty-eight devices and their manufacturers. BMC Medical Informatics and Decision Making,21(1), 166.
11. Koho, I. (2024). Service design handbook prototype for medical device product management. Master's thesis, Haaga-Helia University of Applied Sciences.

How this book came about

The inspiration to write this handbook emerged from a deep faith in the transformative power of service design and the experience of it enriching my work as a medical device product manager. The writing process of this book followed the service design process and mindset, and many service design tools were used during the project. The main process phases included theoretical research, empirical research, and writing and testing.

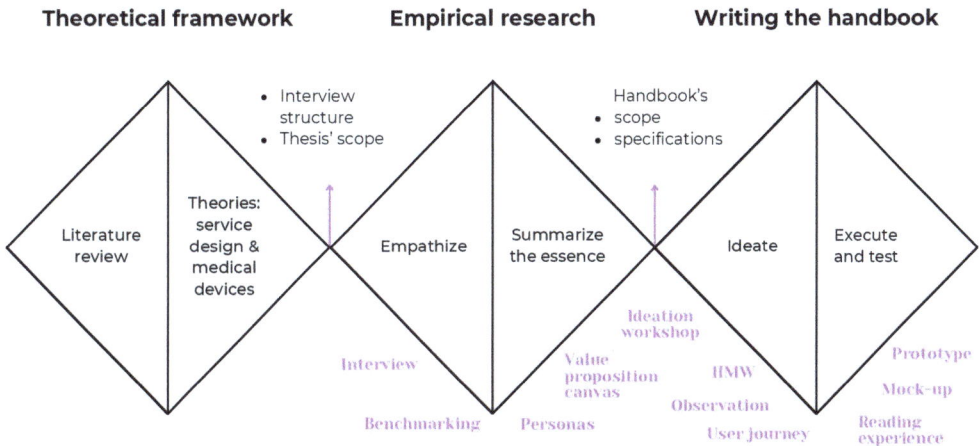

The book is based on the master's thesis *Service Design Handbook Prototype for Medical Device Product Management* (Ida Koho 2024). Its primary objective was to create a needs-driven service design handbook that encourages readers to practice service design to increase user involvement in medical device development.

The theoretical research concluded that service design does not conflict with medical device standards and regulations. It also painted a clear picture of the current benefits and challenges of user involvement in medical device development. They were further investigated in the empirical part that also explored the reasons why service design is not widely used among medical device manufacturers. A lack of awareness and knowledge seems to be a major reason that prevents medical device manufacturers from using human-centered development such as service design.

The primary methods used to empathize with the potential readers were a semi-structured interview with eight experienced medical device product managers in Finland, observations, and prototyping. Both the literature and the empirical data supported the idea of creating a handbook. This sparked the writing process. Antti Brunni contributed as a visitor author, and thanks to him, we could also address software, a crucial part of many medical device businesses. A total of 16 professionals collaborated to create this handbook.

The current state of user involvement

It is common for medical device manufacturers to describe themselves as customer-centric. Having said that, human-centered approaches like service design have yet to catch on in the world of medical devices. There are many reasons (see p. 3) why medical device manufacturers should improve their user involvement – and many as to why it is often not so simple.

Bringing in the voice of the customer and gaining insights on user behavior is often the responsibility of product management. Still, the experience of many product managers is that they have limited time or possibilities to visit the customer for research purposes. In some cases, the product development process completely lacks collaboration with users. The master's thesis (1) behind this book presented the following reasons and attitudes as to why medical device manufacturers do not commonly use human-centered approaches. Can you relate to them?

1. *User involvement is missing in our product development process.*
2. *I'm an old dog, service design was not taught in university.*
3. *We lack knowledge or training on formal methods of user involvement.*
4. *Human (user) emotions should be considered more.*
5. *User involvement sounds very slow.*
6. *We are a technology- and/or product-driven organization.*
7. *I don't have time to visit the customer.*
8. *We work in silos.*
9. *Innovation is appreciated and supported when it occurs in the technical R&D groups.*
10. *I need to figure out how to rename problems as features and turn the features into the company's benefit.*
11. *It's difficult to define a medical device customer or user.*
12. *We use the methods our senior colleagues have found effective in the past.*
13. *The onboarding process for product management was very short.*
14. *I haven't heard about service design.*
15. *The word 'service design' makes me think of service engineers or fashion/interior design.*
16. *There's no time to explore new things (e.g. service design), I'm in survival mode.*
17. *I have so many emails from different consultants (incl. design agencies) coming in that it's not possible to read or reply to all of them.*
18. *I'm not sure if there is a conflict between the service design approach and medical device regulations or quality standards.*
19. *I'm afraid of prototyping because I need to follow regulations.*
20. *It's difficult to understand the (financial) value of service design.*
21. *The perspectives of end users tend to be undervalued, especially when the users are not seen as "clinical champions" (2)*

1. Koho, I. (2024), Service design handbook prototype for medical device product management. Master's thesis, Haaga-Helia University of Applied Sciences.
2. Money, A. G., Barnett, J., Kuljis, J., Craven, M. P., Martin, J. L., & Young, T. (2011). The role of the user within the medical device design and development process: Medical device manufacturers' perspectives. BMC Medical Informatics and Decision Making, 11(1), 15.

Part II

Outlining Service Design

What is service design?

Service design is a human-centered design discipline for innovating intangible things such as services. It's founded on design thinking that considers **the trinity of desirability, feasibility and viability** (IDEO). In the intersection of the three circles exists a **sweet spot** for profitable human-centered innovation.

In 2001, Richard Buchanan (1) outlined the four orders of design that illustrate the capability of design to serve many different purposes. They also show where service design fits in. The picture is modified from the work of Peter Jones (2):

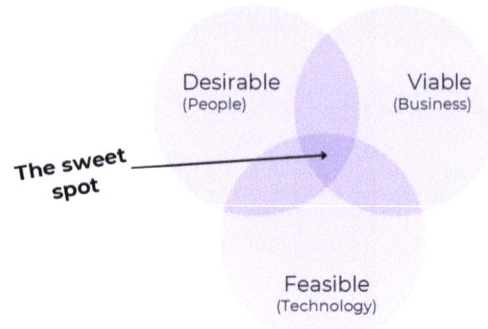

The sweet spot

Desirable (People)

Viable (Business)

Feasible (Technology)

4. Social transformation (complex, unbounded): design for complex societal situations, social systems, policy-making, and community design.

3. Organizational transformation (complex, bounded by business or strategy): change-oriented design of work practices, strategies, and organizational structures.

2. **Products and services**: design for value creation (including service design, product innovation, multichannel, and user experience), design as integrating.

1. Artifacts and communications: design as making, or traditional design practice.

We have a jungle of terminology to describe different design disciplines: service design, experience design, product design, interaction design, UX/UI design, industrial design, business design, futures design, systemic service design, even bio design (3). Built upon the concepts of service design, this book mainly focuses on level 2. However, medical device manufacturers are not an island but a critical part of the healthcare ecosystem. For that reason, some parts of this book discuss aspects related to level 3, such as strategy, systems thinking, and business design. Human-centric design disciplines each have their own characteristics, but they share the same core. It is less significant what you call the approach. What matters is whether you put it into practice or not. But how is that done? Let's move on.

Today's crowded business landscape and emerging customer demands present new challenges for product and service providers. Products need to deliver competitive added value to their users. Customers expect refined services and meaningful experiences. Often, the technology is just a vehicle to facilitate value delivery to the customer.

Service design is an approach for discovering the real need and designing the process of value co-creation. Service design considers the user (or customer, patient, technician, physician) as a human in a certain cultural context. Service design is a systematic approach to deep dive into the user's life and identify patterns and non-verbalized behaviors that can be transformed into a meaningful and/or profitable output. The following quotes from industry pioneers and professionals summarize the essence of service design.

"Service design is a framework and philosophy which emphasizes the customer experience throughout the journey of product utilization"(4)

"Service design is a mindset, a process, a toolset, a cross-disciplinary language and management approach" (5)

"Service design is a comprehensive approach in which user orientation, explorative and creative approaches, visualisation, prototyping and cocreative development play a central role. Service design is on the one hand a process, on the other hand a systematic and methodically supported approach. But above all, it is an attitude that can have a profound influence on the cultures and structures in companies." (6)

In their book **Health Design Thinking** (7), Ku and Lupton explain how healthcare is full of poorly designed devices and products that cause harm to thousands of patients every year. According to them, patients, nurses, doctors, and caregivers are well-positioned to develop concepts for better products but often lack the know-how to bring their ideas to life. Designing a medical device is a collaboration of multiple professionals, and a product manager equipped with human-centered design knowledge can play an important part in designing the added value.

You may already be using tools or elements of service design—and that's an excellent first step! However, adopting an approach goes beyond simply selecting methods or techniques. In the following chapters, we'll explore service design through three lenses: as a process, a mindset, and a toolbox. Afterward, you'll find practical suggestions on how and where product managers can leverage the benefits of service design.

1. Buchanan, R. (2001). Design Research and the New Learning. Design Issues, 17(4), 3–23.
2. Jones, P. H. (2014). Systemic design principles for complex social systems. In: Metcalf, G. (eds.). Social Systems and Design. Translational Systems Sciences, vol 1. Springer.
3. Dade-Robertson, M., & Zhang, M. (2024). Theory and design in the biotechnical age: A schematic understanding of Bio Design and Synthetic Biology practice. The Design Journal, 27(5), 800–822.
4. Hamid, U. Z. A., & Suoheimo, M. (2023). Product development challenges for emerging technologies and service design roles in addressing the issues. In: Umar Zakir Abdul Hamid, & Mari Suoheimo (eds.). Service Design for Emerging Technologies Product Development: Bridging the Interdisciplinary Knowledge Gap, pp. 9–22. Springer.
5. Stickdorn, M., Hormess, M. E., Lawrence, A., & Schneider, J. (2018). This is Service Design Doing: Applying Service Design Thinking in the Real World – A Practitioners' Handbook (first edition). O'Reilly.
6. Mager, B., Sistig, M., Chen, Y., Ruiz, K., & Corona, C. (2020). The Future of Service Design. Service Design Network.
7. Ku, B., & Lupton, E. (2022). Health Design Thinking: Creating Products and Services for Better Health (second edition). The MIT Press.

Service design as a process

The process of service design should be considered a framework rather than a detailed step-by-step process description. It is meant to facilitate your design project, not restrict it. The service design process should not replace any medical device development processes that have been created to fulfill the ISO 13485 standard for medical devices or local regulations. Instead, the service design process, mindset and tools are supplementary assets to assist you in involving the users and customers in the development. In an ideal case, the process will help you create human-centered, effective and profitable medical device products and services. This chapter, as the entire book, is best read with a willingness to re-evaluate your current working methods.

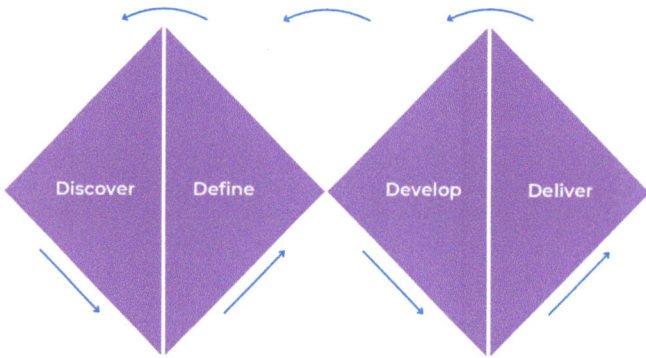

As the double diamonds above illustrate, service design is an explorative and iterative, non-linear process. The **arrows ponting up and down** show if the nature of the phase is divergent (the diamond opens) or convergent (the diamond closes). In a divergent phase, the amount of information, ideas, or data increases. The phase employs the so called "yes, and..." mentality, meaning no idea should be shot down at this point; instead, you should try to build on top of the ideas of others. This is the time to mute your inner critic.

A convergent phase, the right side of a diamond, is about filtering and summarizing the generated data. While the amount of information decreases, the aim is to crystallize and concretize an idea, problem statement, solution, or concept of a product or service. Here we enter the so called "yes, but..." mode and apply a suitable decision-making process. According to the book **This is Service Design Doing (TiSDD)**, divergent thinking and doing is all about seeking opportunities, while convergent is about making decisions (3).

The **arrows above** the diamods describe the iterative nature of the process. TiSDD describes service design as "an exploratory, adaptive and experimental approach, iterating toward implementation."(3)

The magic of the service design process happens **between the two diamonds** when the right problem has been identified and defined. It's important not to jump to the solution too early. When you take care to nail the first diamond, you will not waste time fixing the wrong problem.

Only after the first diamond, can we start the famous ideation. Typically, a workshop is arranged to gather creative minds and experts from different fields. When we have collected plenty of ideas, we try to push for a few more. A good idea is more likely found in a pool of fifty ideas than of a dozen!

Eventually, selected **ideas or concepts are tested** in collaboration with the customer. Finally, prototyping and readjustments will result in a solution to the defined problem. There are different types of prototyping: you may aim to get the buy-in from investors or simply seek to know the answers yourself. Don't prolong preparing the first low-fidelity prototypes – you might end up burning resources.

Example: Planning a design project
Improvement of laboratory device delivery

The example below illustrates a process of improving device delivery using the service design approach. The scope of the scenario covers customers who have decided to place an order and expect the medical device to be delivered.

- Completing the first diamond results in precious information about user behavior and needs which will be reflected throughout the rest of the process. The user will be involved in all steps where possible.
- The second diamond results in a needs-driven delivery process that is tested with the customer and implemented.

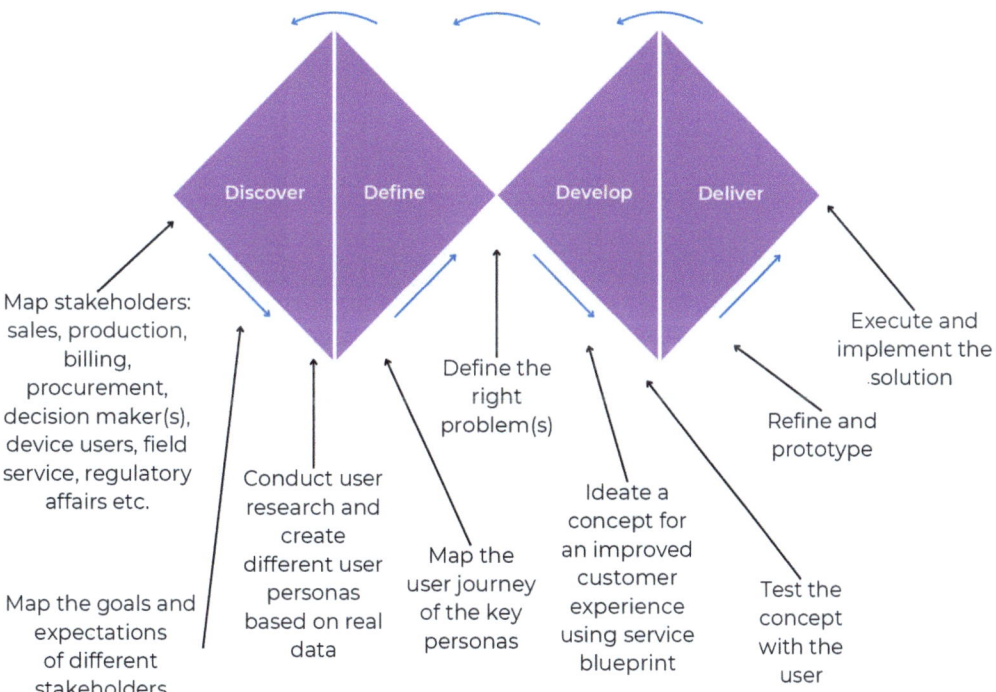

The process should adapt to fit the problem, not the other way around

In an ideal case, the service design process guides the project towards solving the right problem and then solving the problem right. The classic double diamond by the Design Council (1) is probably one of the most popular ways to describe the service design process, but it's not the only one. IDEO (2) summarizes the design process in three steps: inspiration, ideation, and implementation. Stefan Moritz (4), on the other hand, suggests six steps: understanding, thinking, generating, filtering, explaining, and realizing. What's common for all processes is that they are iterative; they do not start with ideation but with research, and implementation involves prototyping with the user. Another important detail is that the process should adapt to fit the problem, not the other way around (3). A good example of this is the triple diamond that was used to create this handbook (see page 5). For systemic challenges, check the Design Council's (1) extended version of the double diamond.

Design Thinking by Tim Brown

"The design process is best described metaphorically as a system of spaces rather than a pre-defined series of orderly steps. The spaces demarcate different sorts of related activities that together form the continuum of innovation. Design thinking can feel chaotic to those experiencing it for the first time. But over the life of a project participants come to see – as they did at Kaiser – that the process makes sense and achieves results, even though its architecture differs from the linear, milestone-based processes typical of other kinds of business activities." (5)

Kaiser Permanente is a large American non-profit healthcare provider that improved patient experience, nurses' job satisfaction, and productivity through design thinking when collaborating with Tim Brown and IDEO.

The fussy front end is the chaotic phase of the design process. At this stage, information is unorganized and elements have yet to find their places. Over time, clarity will emerge.

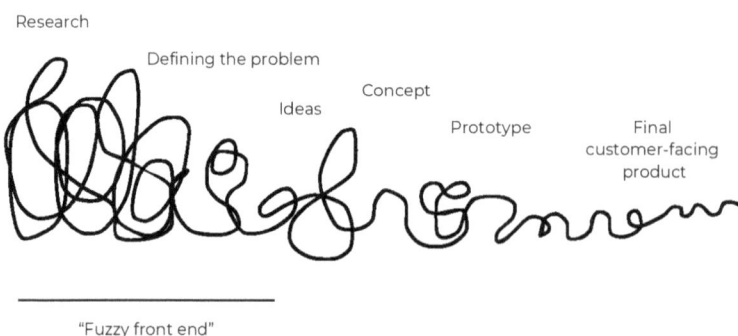

Research

Defining the problem

Ideas

Concept

Prototype

Final customer-facing product

"Fuzzy front end"

Design ~~for~~ the customer
Design with the customer

The abundance of user research data may make you feel overwhelmed at first, but there are many tools to help you organize data with your team. One example is the empathy map. In addition to organizing interview or observation data, it helps discover opportunities and empathize with the customer.

The Empathy Map	
Says	**Thinks**
"It's easy to order consumables for this device."	"I wish someone would do the consumable inventory for me today."
Does	**Feels**
Spends an hour doing the inventory before ordering the consumables.	Feels comfortable with a local food delivery app type user experience.

Service design is an approach and a philosophy. The process is only one part of it. The next page gives you a list of tips on service design tools. The following chapter, on the other hand, explains the service design mindset and principles.

1. designcouncil.org.uk
2. IDEO.org (2015). The Field Guide to Human-Centered Design.
3. .Stickdorn, M., Lawrence, A., Hormess, M. E., & Schneider, J. (2018). This is Service Design Doing: Applying Service Design Thinking in the Real World – A Practitioners' Handbook (first edition). O'Reilly.
4. Moritz, S. (2005). Service Design: Practical Access to an Evolving Field.
5. Brown, T. (2008). Design Thinking. Harvard Business Review.

Service design as a toolbox

There is an abundance of service design tools for all sorts of purposes, with new tools constantly emerging. A tool or method doesn't need to be new and fancy to be effective; in fact, classic approaches like customer interviews remain unbeatable, especially when product developers participate directly, fostering empathy with users (1). A good tool serves its purpose without creating confusion or overlapping with other tools.

To be able to use the service design approach, you don't need to be familiar with every possible tool out there. The set of tools provided in Part V of this book should get you off to a good start. The more you practice service design, the more you will understand which tool fits which purpose and how to use them to their full potential.

Many tools serve various phases of service design. The customer journey map and business model canvas, for example, are great for defining problems, ideating, developing, or communicating.

Source examples

Servicedesigntools.org has descriptions of different tools as well as a downloadable tutorial for collaborating with stakeholders in a healthcare design project, complete with a toolkit.

Designabetterbusiness.tools offers tools specifically for business design and may help you discover new business opportunities.

Thisisservicedesigndoing.com/methods includes hands-on descriptions of methods for research, ideation, prototyping, and facilitation. The page is a free online version of the book This is Service Design Methods.

Service Design: Practical Access to an Evolving Field, a free e-book by Stefan Moritz (2005), provides a comprehensive list of service design tools for each phase of the service design process.

Strategyzer.com lists service design tools and case examples.

The Hyper Island Toolbox has a set of activities for creativity, teamwork, self-leadership, innovation, facilitation, well-being, and DEIB (diversity, equity, inclusion, and belonging).

Digital white boards such as **Miro, Mural** and **Figma** are excellent sources for discovering tools.

1. Ulla Jones – palvelumuotoilun moniosaajan kasvutarina. Palvelumuotoilun kasvutarinoita podcast, episode 6. March 8, 2021.

Service design as a mindset

Service design is not only a process or a set of tools but a systematic approach, philosophy, and attitude that follows certain principles. It's far from rocket science, but still, adopting the mindset and working culture may require practice. The boxes below present and compare service design principles as listed by two significant sources.

Service design principles by the Design Council (1)	Service design principles by TiSDD (2)
1. **Be people-centered** 2. **Communicate visually and inclusively** 3. **Collaborate & co-create** 4. Iterate, Iterate, Iterate	1. **Human-centered** 2. **Collaborative** 3. Iterative 4. **Sequencial** 5. Real 6. **Holistic**

Occasionally, a medical device product manager may need to take on the role of a facilitator or researcher and abandon the position of an expert. For those moments, the Design Council (1) provides a great checklist with its seven tenets of service design:

1. Get past your own great idea
2. Don't be restricted by your own knowledge
3. Spend time with real people in real environments
4. Identify other users
5. Follow your users' lead and needs
6. Think about the whole journey of the product
7. Prototype and test your idea

TIPS for further exploration of the service design mindset and philosophy

It's easy to lose your way in the abundance of material related to different design disciplines. Start simple by checking out these two:
1. **The design process and principles:** the Design Council (1) provides clear videos and other content about the design process and principles. Study the Double Diamond and its extended version for systemic challenges.
2. **Real-life examples:** IDEO (3) has published (service) design case examples on medical devices.

The following pages describe the essential elements of the service design approach: human-centricity, holism, collaboration, and the power of visualization.

Human-centered design

Empathy is a vital skill when approaching problems from a human-centered perspective. Empathy is the superpower of a designer, but could it be that for a product manager, too?

Tim Brown describes the benefits of empathy in design: "One can imagine the world from multiple perspectives. By taking a 'people first' approach, design thinkers can imagine solutions that are inherently desirable and meet explicit or latent needs." (4)

Medical device regulations and ISO 13485 place the user at the center but are limited to good intentions and high-level requirements. (5) Many manufacturers could benefit from employing a practical, human-centered approach and finding doers who can put it into practice.

As Juuso and Seppänen phrase it: "The beauty of medical device development is that it's all standardized and governed by regulations but what your user (customer) actually wants will guide you in selecting the correct requirements and processes." (5)

Whose needs and abilities should you address?
A human-centered approach can be employed in product and service development, leadership, strategy, and more. Your goal and "customer" define if you call your approach customer-centered, user-centered, employee-centered, patient-centered, planet-centered, or equity-centered – to give a few examples. There may not even be a need to put a label on it in the first place! It's also important to note that while a veterinary product manager might take a pet-centered approach, it doesn't mean they are anti-human.

The medical device product manager is often responsible for translating the customer's needs to the rest of the development team. To do that, it's important to go to the customer, live their everyday life, observe patterns and become aware of behaviors that may not be verbalized.

When designing products and services, your customer's needs are your priority, but in addition, you must consider other parties affected by the service (2). In the context of healthcare, these might be parents, caregivers, procurement, logistics, and so on. Next, we will take a holistic perspective to design.

1. designcouncil.org.uk
2. Stickdorn, M., Lawrence, A., Hormess, M. E., & Schneider, J. (2018). This is Service Design Doing: Applying Service Design Thinking in the Real World – A Practitioners' Handbook (first edition). O'Reilly.
3. IDEO.org
4. Brown, T. (2008) Design Thinking. Harvard Business Review.
5. Juuso, I. & Seppänen, T. (2023). How the service design approach can empower medical device development to reach its user-centered goals. In: Umar Zakir Abdul Hamid, & Mari Suoheimo (eds.). Service Design for Emerging Technologies Product Development: Bridging The Interdisciplinary Knowledge Gap, pp. 101–115. Springer.

Holistic design

Service design is a holistic approach – and in medicine, holism is already a familiar concept. It's usually beneficial to consider the whole body instead of treating separate parts of it, as the parts are most often interconnected. Similarly, service design aims to assess the use of a service or a product as a whole rather than look at individual steps or functions. As TiSDD summarizes: "Services should sustainably address the needs of all stakeholders through the entire service and across the business." (3)

A real-life example of holism
One great example of service design related to medical devices is the story of Doug Dietz, a GE industrial designer whose iterations on an MRI imaging device utilizing empathy and holistic thinking demonstrate the clinical impact design can create. The first version of Doug's imaging device looked scary to pediatric patients and caused anxiety. Improved, playful versions increased patient satisfaction up to 90%. In addition to children, the design process considered parents. One MRI room design included (fake) piña coladas for the parents. The detail made the parents smile, and their state of mind affected their child, which had a further positive impact on the imaging process and the work of healthcare professionals. This example not only shows how a holistic approach enables innovation but also demonstrates the importance of human emotions in the design process.

Services can be visualized through a linear **customer journey map** (page 59) or a **service blueprint** (page 21), which aids holistic thinking and helps consider different stakeholders and emotions. However, the value network of the healthcare ecosystem is complex, and sometimes linear thinking falls short.

Systemic service design differs from holistic service design in e.g. the scope of research and action and the amount of perspectives considered. When working with systemic challenges, **stakeholder mapping** (page 22), **ecosystem mapping** or **value mapping** may help you see if you have considered all stakeholders and opportunities.

Watch the TED talk about this story or read about it on ideou.com or thisisdesignthinking. net by searching for **Doug Dietz**

Systems thinking according to WHO

*"Systems thinking works to reveal the underlying characteristics and relationships of systems. Work in fields as diverse as engineering, economics and ecology shows systems to be constantly changing, with components that are tightly connected and highly sensitive to change elsewhere in the system. They are **non-linear, unpredictable and resistant to change, with seemingly obvious solutions sometimes worsening a problem**."* (2) Typical health-related examples that require systems thinking include tobacco use, obesity, and the battle against emerging pathogen (e.g. tuberculosis, COVID19).

Monat and Gannon conclude that "systems thinking is the opposite of linear thinking and (…) focuses on the relationships among system components, as opposed to the components themselves. It is holistic (integrative) thinking instead of analytic (dissective) thinking." (1)

Systems thinking isn't suited to all challenges. It also doesn't replace other thinking approaches but rather supplements analytic and statistical thinking.

The Iceberg Model below shows how both visible and hidden factors impact a system. Both illustrations on this page are modified from Monat et al. (2015).

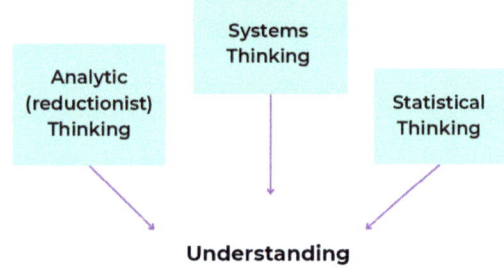

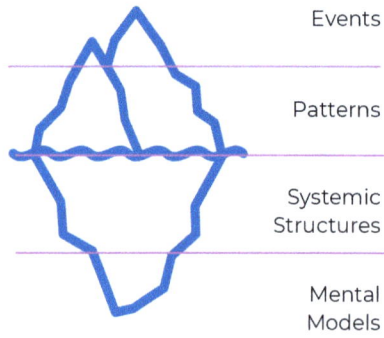

Events

Patterns

Systemic
Structures

Mental
Models

TIP!

Systemsorienteddesign.net and **systemic-design.org** are examples of sources for learning more about systems thinking, systemic design, related tools as well as frameworks and gigamapping.
Thesystemsthinker.com also includes literature related to healthcare.

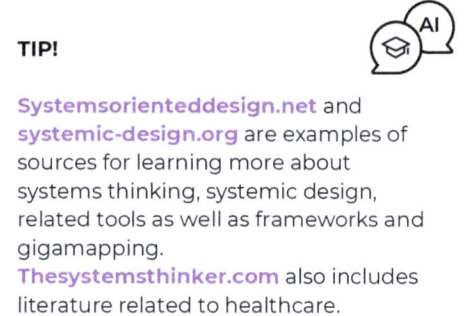

A service should be designed with different stakeholders and the physical and cultural environment in mind. Additionally, the customer's service experience should be consistent across touchpoints. The website, user interface, and product insert should all give the user the same feeling. The customers don't care about the single touchpoints, but they experience the service or product in totality and evaluate its functionality based on how it all works together and provides value to them. (4)

A holistic way of designing often requires experts working together as well as the involvement of users. Next, let's talk about collaboration.

1. Monat, J. P., & Gannon, T. F. (2015). What is systems thinking? A review of selected literature plus recommendations. American Journal of Systems Science, 4(1), 11–26.
2. Don de Savigny, & Taghreed Adam (eds.) (2009). Systems Thinking for Health Systems Strengthening. World Health Organization.
3. Stickdorn, M., Lawrence, A., Hormess, M. E., & Schneider, J. (2018). This is Service Design Doing: Applying Service Design Thinking in the Real World – A Practitioners' Handbook (first edition). O'Reilly.
4. Penin, L. (2018). An Introduction to Service Design: Designing the Invisible. Bloomsbury Visual Arts.

Collaborate and co-create

Service design is a collaborative approach that shakes up the old customs around expertise. The service designer's mindset makes the user the expert on the service. The company experts may know a lot, but the customer is the real expert on their own life and should thus be interviewed and observed.

"The increasing complexity of products, services, and experiences has replaced the myth of the lone creative genius with the reality of the enthusiastic interdisciplinary collaborator."

Tim Brown (1)

"Stakeholders of various backgrounds and functions should be actively engaged in the service design process."

This is Service Design Doing (2)

Design Thinking for Health

Designthinkingforhealth.org has a set of videos to teach design thinking in the context of healthcare. The content is created by the University of Pennsylvania School of Nursing and the Rita and Alex Hillman Foundation. The course is targeted at nurses instead of medical device manufacturers, but the introduction videos provide an easy access to the steps of the design thinking process in a healthcare setting.

On the website, Mary Marion Leary from Penn Nursing states, "To me, innovation is not just one thing, it's not just technology, it's not just medical devices. Innovation is also solving problems in a way that adds value and creating different strategies and implementing them in different ways. Innovation also includes how we communicate with each other, with our patients, other colleagues, and how we get information out to the broader public."

(Website accessed in July 2024)

Collaboration requires good communication, and visualizations help communicate and interpret problems, concepts, and results. Real photos transmit the emotional aspects as well as support and provide evidence for verbal research data. Let's move on to talking about service design's superpower – visualization.

1. Brown, T. (2008). Design Thinking. Harvard Business Review.
2. Stickdorn, M., Lawrence, A., Hormess, M. E., & Schneider, J. (2018). This is Service Design Doing: Applying Service Design Thinking in the Real World – A Practitioners' Handbook (first edition). O'Reilly.
3. Ku, B., & Lupton, E. (2022). Health Design Thinking: Creating Products and Services for Better Health (second edition). The MIT Press.

The power of visualization

Service design strongly relies on the visualization of invisible things when it comes to communication, decision-making, and innovation. However, it doesn't mean that a product manager using the service design approach needs to be a visual artist. Many digital tools (Canva, Figma, Miro, Mural, Stormboard, LucidSpark) require zero drawing skills and still help you illustrate the intangible for your colleagues or for yourself. A few boxes or sticky notes and a couple of different colors are sometimes worth a thousand words.

Digital whiteboards have plenty of templates for different purposes such as mapping scenarios, sequencing a linear set of actions, making decisions, and solving problems. These platforms are constantly updated, and new tools emerge. Explore the different tools with relevant keywords, e.g. 'value', 'problem', or 'matrix'.

This chapter presents a couple of visualization tools to help explain concepts, illustrate text, boost creativity, sequence events, understand complex systems and relations between people and things, or ensure everyone is on the same page. More tools are presented in Part V.

The Now-How-Wow tool by Gamestorming is an example of a simple but efficient visualization tool for categorizing ideas on a matrix. You could use it to organize ideas created in a workshop.

Example: Decreasing user errors

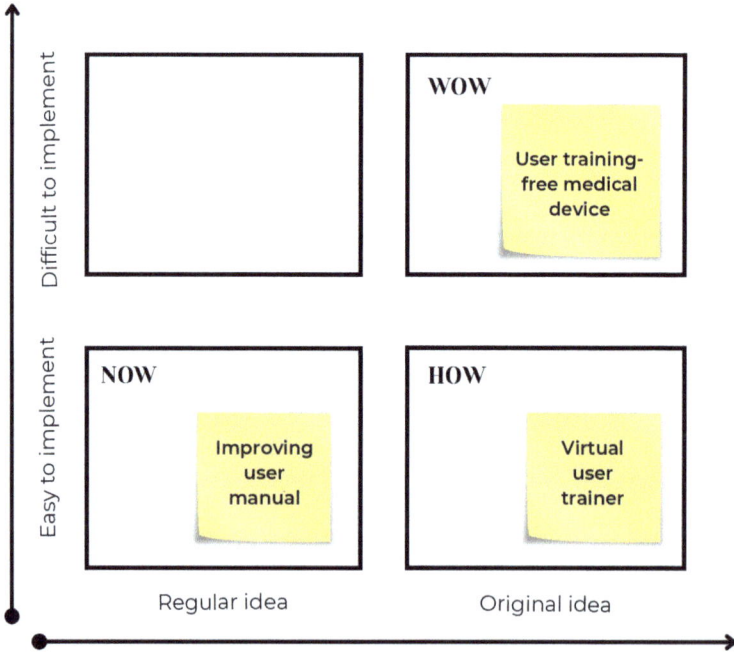

Service blueprint

A service blueprint is a practical tool for visualizing and orchestrating a sequence of (intangible) interrelated actions (1). Its purpose is to show the main touchpoints between the provider and the user and name elements that impact or support the user experience and value creation. It helps medical device product managers and their colleagues with ideation, development, and communication tasks. It's a great tool for optimizing processes and eliminating redundancy (2). A service blueprint is an extended version of the user journey (page 59) that considers the frontstage (visible to the user) and backstage (not visible to the user) of the process.

Scoping the problem is important. For example, consumable ordering, technical troubleshooting, and new device delivery all require their own blueprint. Visualizing the journey, the sequence of actions and touchpoints helps design a detailed sequence in a holistic way. Remember, **the customer will experience the service as a whole rather than as a sequence of individual steps** (3).

Example:
Service blueprint: Remote troubleshooting of an IVD device

Time	0 min	5 min	15-30 min	40 min	120 min	160 min
Touchpoint	Website	Phone	Device	Mail/phone	Mail/phone	Mail/phone
Customer action	Problem --> searches for contact information	Calls service number & describes the problem	Waits for the next steps	Receives first trouble-shooting results and questions	Co-trouble-shooting with field service	Problem solved, case closed
	The processing of clinical samples comes to a halt. Are replacements available?					
Frontstage actions (Distributor, field service, sales?) *Visible to the customer*	Contact info easily accessible	Evaluating the need for further assistance with the manufact.	Device's remote control activities	Communicates in a local language	Communicates in a local language	Delivering result
Invisible to the customer **Backstage actions (Manufacturer)**	-	Planning the diagnostic route and activities	First-level trouble-shooting	First-level diagnosis and further questions	Trouble-shooting continues	Diagnosis and fix
Supportive actions			Software help desk on demand	Software help desk on demand	R&D support on demand	

1. Stickdorn, M., Lawrence, A., Hormess, M. E., & Schneider, J. 2018. This is Service Design Doing: Applying Service Design Thinking in the Real World – A Practitioners' Handbook (first edition). O'Reilly.
2. Gibbons, S. (2017). Service blueprints: definition. NN Group.
3. Penin, L. (2018). An Introduction to Service Design: Designing the Invisible. Bloomsbury Visual Arts.

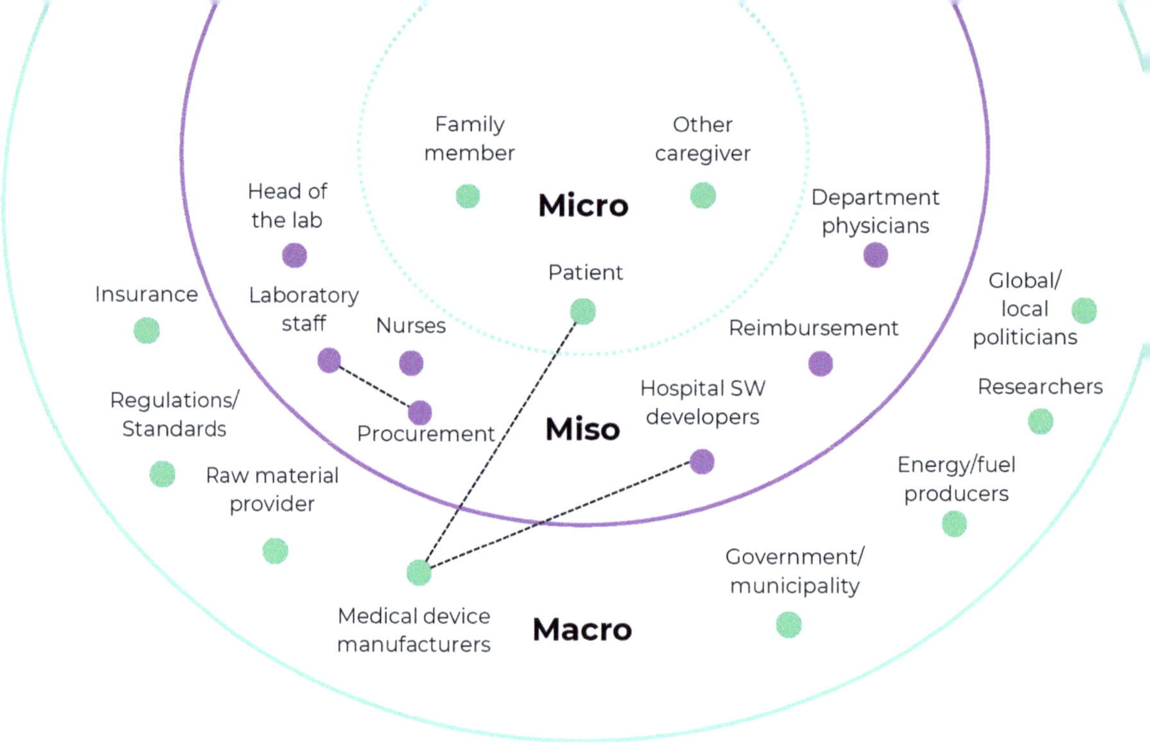

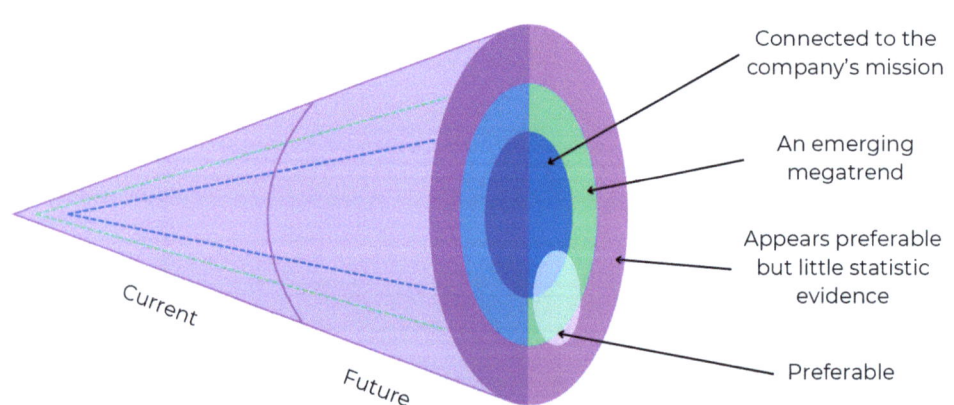

Micro

Family member

Other caregiver

Head of the lab

Department physicians

Insurance

Laboratory staff

Nurses

Patient

Global/ local politicians

Regulations/ Standards

Reimbursement

Researchers

Procurement

Miso

Hospital SW developers

Raw material provider

Energy/fuel producers

Medical device manufacturers

Macro

Government/ municipality

Smaply is one of many digital tools available for **stakeholder mapping**. On their website, they provide a comprehensive explanation of the mapping process and its purpose, including a helpful video.

Connected to the company's mission

An emerging megatrend

Appears preferable but little statistic evidence

Preferable

Current

Future

Illustration of a future scenario derived from customer feedback, inspired by **Joseph Voros' Futures Cone** (1). The original layers are labeled Possible, Plausible, Probable, and Preferable.

1. Voros, J. (2017). Big history and anticipation. In: Poli, R. (ed.). Handbook of Anticipation. Springer.

Visualizing your own thoughts allows you to effortlessly zoom in on details or take a step back for a broader, more strategic perspective on your projects or challenges. Digital whiteboards make the transition seamless and provide more or less automated illustration tools, so no drawing skills are required. Visualization can be used for more than deliverables.

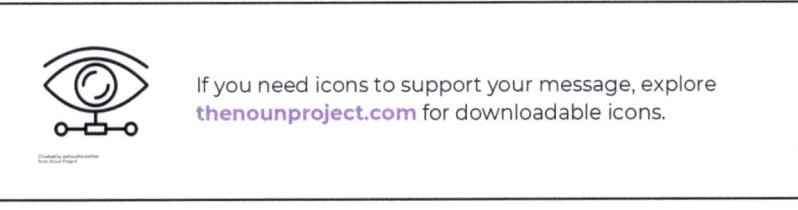

If you need icons to support your message, explore thenounproject.com for downloadable icons.

The previous examples showcase various types of visualization, aiming to inspire and empower you to integrate visual elements into your work. Visual tools are also powerful for storytelling as they make complex ideas relatable and memorable. What kind of visualization would help you in your situation – linear or non-linear? What do you wish to do: connect dots, define patterns, demonstrate, organize your thoughts, or communicate?

Utilizing visualizations in product development and management processes

By Antti Brunni

Visualization plays a crucial role in conveying complex information clearly. If there is one aspect of design that significantly aids in the adoption of design outcomes, it is visualization. Whether presenting strategic or detailed information, visualizing data allows more people to process and engage with it effectively. Visualization serves as a communication tool, enabling recipients to understand information better and, for example, ask clarifying questions.

Benefits of visualization for the product manager
In the role of a product manager, visualization can be beneficial in the following contexts:

1. Improved decision-making through clarity
Visualization converts complex information into a format that is easier to comprehend. When involving others in decision-making, it is undoubtedly the most effective means. By visually presenting key metrics such as safety and product performance indicators, a product manager can better communicate their plans and needs for resources. Discussions based on visualized information are invaluable in co-design processes: "I'll show you our design, and you can explain how you understand it and what should be modified to make it valuable for you."

Remember, well-executed design work can mitigate risks to some extent.

2. Enhanced stakeholder communication
Using visualizations as a part of the design process output promotes more effective communication among stakeholders, such as regulatory experts, clinical specialists, and developers. Visual tools help these groups better understand risks and identify areas of improvement, which fosters more efficient collaboration. Product managers can use visual techniques to present regulatory requirements, development progress, or market shifts. When creating digital solutions, visualizations serve as the first tangible outputs.

3. Multilevel visualization for enhanced insights

Visualization techniques can be applied across different levels to meet the needs of various audiences:

- High-level summaries: Charts and dashboards offer stakeholders, such as executives or customers, a quick overview by visually summarizing key risks or performance indicators.
- Detailed data presentations: In-depth visualizations, such as risk matrices or line charts, allow a closer examination of specific risks or system components. These are useful for technical teams involved in implementation and product refinement.
- Contextual visual aids: Visualization tools provide decision-making aids in context, e.g. when comparing patient outcomes. This supports an understanding of not only risks but also potential benefits, promoting balanced product decision-making.

4. Simplified regulatory compliance

Visualization facilitates transparency in the risk assessment of product requirements, making it accessible to auditors and regulatory bodies. Graphical representations of user feedback, risk management actions, and compliance checklists streamline reporting and clarify the product's safety profile. Bear in mind that if your product includes digital features or interfaces, they are often subject to testing, the documentation of which aids in risk identification.

Examples of visualization types for product managers

- Vision images and graphical goal maps
- Visualized summaries of co-design and testing: These allow product managers to assess which risks require attention or mitigation.
- Risk visualization: Consider depicting product-related risks as a staircase where risks are categorized by impact. Could this foster a shared understanding of which development actions are the most critical?
- Tables and data visualization: If managing or communicating large volumes of data related to product management or development is challenging, try visualizing the information and assess feedback from others on data comprehensibility and discussion quality.

Conclusions: integrating visualization for added value

Integrating visualization into design and product management processes allows product managers to seamlessly engage with various facets of product development. It provides an effective means to simplify complex information, ensure risks are clearly understood during decision-making, and improve communication between stakeholders. Visualization not only aids in day-to-day management but also enhances the product manager's strategic value by enabling effective and impactful risk communication, ultimately contributing to the product's success in the market.

Part III

Service Design for Medical Device Product Management

Product manager's checklist

This is a product manager's service design task checklist for beginners. Try to collect all tasks while reading or after reading this book.

- [x] Read a service design book

- [ ] Watch a video about service design, design thinking, or the service design process.

- [ ] To figure out how service design has been used with products like yours, do a couple of searches using Google, Google Scholar, or an academic database. Use at least [service design] or [user involvement] + [your product type] or [clinical condition/event] in your search.
  - Example 1: Service design case study + blood glucose meter (or diabetes)
  - Example 2: User involvement + CT imaging (or scanning experience)

  Don't expect too many relevant results. It's likely that there are no publications about your specific product type. You can be the first to make one!

- [ ] Fill in the user persona template (see pages 56–58). Contemplate the data you enter. Is it based on
  - a user interview
  - another formal method like observation or ethnography
  - your own or your colleague's assumptions
  - second-hand input?

- [ ] Prepare a user journey (page 59) or service blueprint (page 21) for your selected user persona (find an instruction video if needed).

- [ ] Take a course on service design (there are plenty of options available!)

- [ ] Think about a project you could do to practice the service design process. The user or customer in your first project could be a paying customer, your colleague, your boss, a partner, a family member, or a friend. Find inspiration on page 29.

- [ ] Visit your customer in their environment.

Using service design as a product manager

Service design can be used to bring about change, invention, or innovation. Instead of just trading goods, providers these days co-produce experiences and co-create value with the customer or consumer. The service design approach is a great way to design the invisible aspects of a product. These are the top three purposes for which a medical device product manager could use service design and design thinking:

1. Service design is a way to get closer to the customer's life, whether they are your colleague, a paying customer, or another stakeholder. Service design may help increase user involvement throughout the product development journey and ensure that design input is based on actual customer needs.
2. Delivering a medical device product/service is a sequence of interrelated actions that requires the collaboration and effort of several people. A product manager often bounces between **frontstage** (visible to the customer) and **backstage** (invisible to the customer) duties. Visualization tools such as service blueprint (see page 21) help grasp a complex sequence of actions (touchpoints) both frontstage and backstage.
3. Collaboration, decision making and successful product development and delivery cannot happen without a solid strategy. Design thinking is an effective way to produce one.

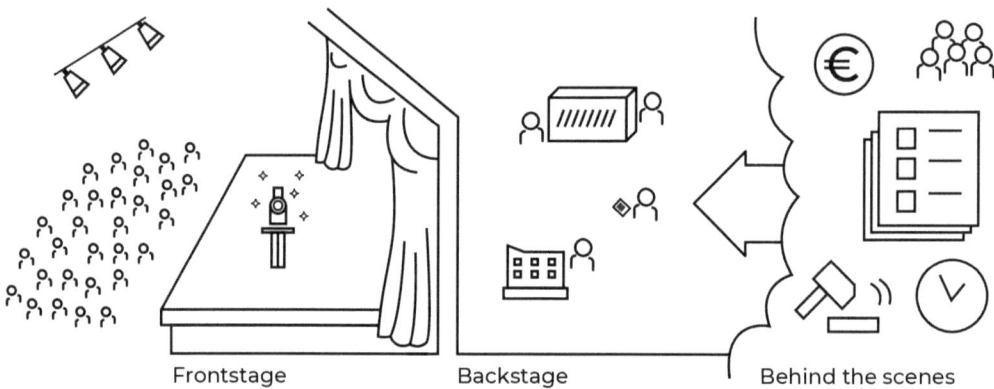

Frontstage   Backstage   Behind the scenes

This chapter provides ideas on where a product manager could use the service design approach. Please note that the responsibilities and tasks of product management vary greatly depending on the organization type and size as well as the product type and its maturity. A product manager's job description based on interviews of eight IVD medical device product managers can be found at the end of the handbook (pages 82–83). Also, in this chapter, Antti Brunni explains what's different when your medical device is software.

The picture is modified from Miller, M. & Flowers, E. (2016). The difference between a journey map and a service blueprint. Practical by Design.

Examples of projects or problems the service design approach can come in handy with

- Optimizing product use, service consumption, or customer experience
- Understanding what patient sample logistics look like within the hospital
- Understanding details such as how a healthcare professional needs to transport/store/clean your device in the hospital
- Creating a user-needs-driven manual or introduction video
- Target-group-specific advertising (**Traditional marketing vs. service design by Smaply**)
- What happens in an ambulance during patient transfer and what value does your product deliver in that setting?
- Understanding the value of a device/service for an elderly customer at home
- Underdiagnosis of a condition as a challenge (IDEO's case on Alzheimer's)
- Usability, ergonomics, and user experience of a physical product or package
- Sales process or a customer support or purchase workflow
- Improving treatment adherence, care, or convenience
- Discovering invisible barriers to device use such as culture, emotions (shame, fear), or attitudes
- Creating and implementing a brand strategy, product strategy, or launch strategy
- Identifying opportunities or challenges
- Building a product training material and event
- Customer feedback processing and other post-market surveillance tasks
- Preparing the workflow for fixing product delivery issues to maximize customer satisfaction (e.g. replacements, compensation, or other information)
- Mapping the customer procurement process
- Mapping the user journey for risk analysis

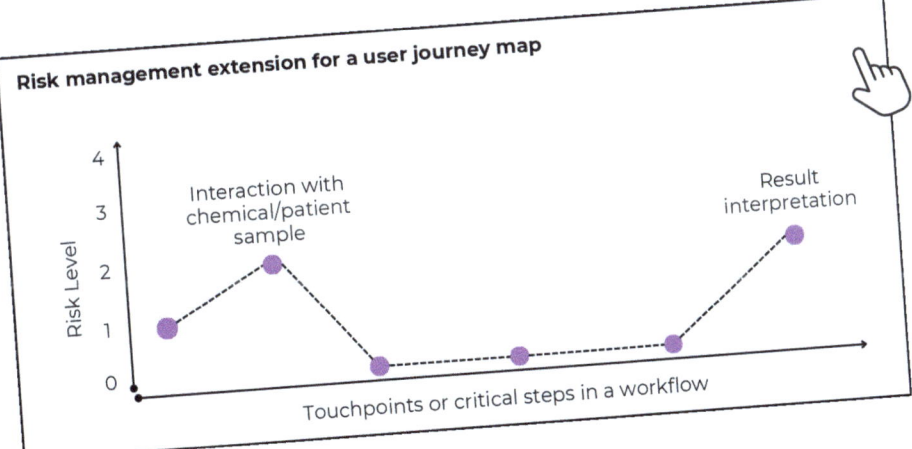

You can extend the user journey map with risk analysis. The numeric scale of risk severity in this example is an imaginary scale. Read more about **customer journey** mapping on page 59.

Service design & product development

This book does not suggest replacing your current medical device product development process with the service design process in this way:

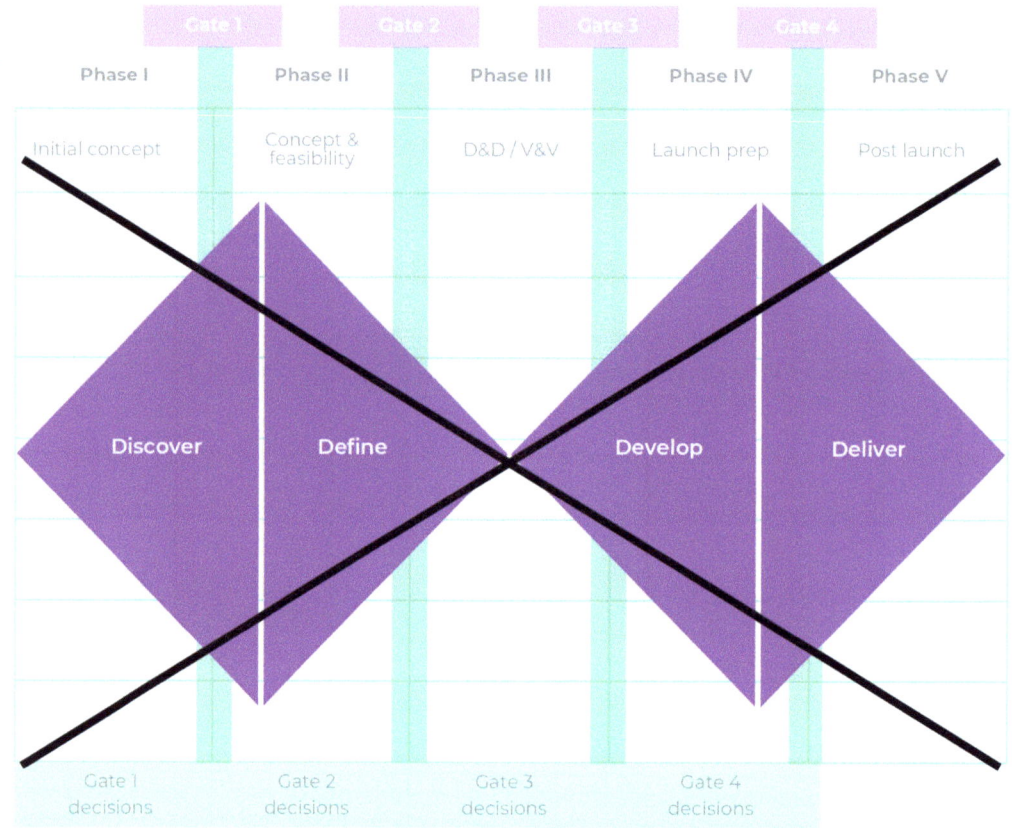

Instead, this handbook suggests that the service design approach provides practical assistance for co-creating with people (e.g. users, customers) to understand their needs better and deliver a solution that fits its purpose.

When service design is integrated in the company culture, the stage-gate process of product development governed by standards and regulations could look like this:

This illustration is not a framework you can copy and paste; instead, it aims to visualize the usefulness of service design for product development projects big and small. Service design is an excellent approach for projects that require qualitative methods.

The product manager's contribution to product development depends on the maturity of the product as well as several other factors. Many of their daily tasks and challenges are not directly connected to product development. Let's zoom out for a minute and do a positioning exercise.

Where are you today and where are you heading?

To explore the world through a service lens and locate our offering, we'll use the map of macro-trend models with service systems by Lee et al. Think of a product, service, or offering that you currently work with and study the map next page. **Where does your offering stand in this universe of services?** You can take the perspective of a first-level customer (e.g. distributor, patient, or nurse) or a second-level customer (e.g. patient, laboratory technician, or hospital procurement).

The x-axis

Left: A people-centered model refers to when customers are served by people such as nurses, key account managers, or service engineers. At this end of the spectrum, human connection creates a sense of privilege.

Right: In a technology-centered model, labor costs and service resources are cut by using technology. Health service chatbots, AI-based therapists, and drug delivery robots are examples of technology replacing human labor.

Hybrid model: Self-service is used by the service providers to empower the customer to make their own decisions. Examples of this are glucose monitoring devices or self-check-in devices in hospitals.

The y-axis

Product design covers the visible part of the service system, e.g. an ultrasound device, a robot, or architectural spaces such as hospitals or laboratories.
Experience design, on the other hand, relates to the non-visible part of the service system that includes people's feelings, perceptions, the atmosphere in the environment, or activities hosted in public spaces.
Service design connects, activates and communicates between the two service systems to generate benefit and create value out of the services.

The z-axis

There are no right or wrong places to be; different models simply deliver different customer experiences. Where are you headed in the future?

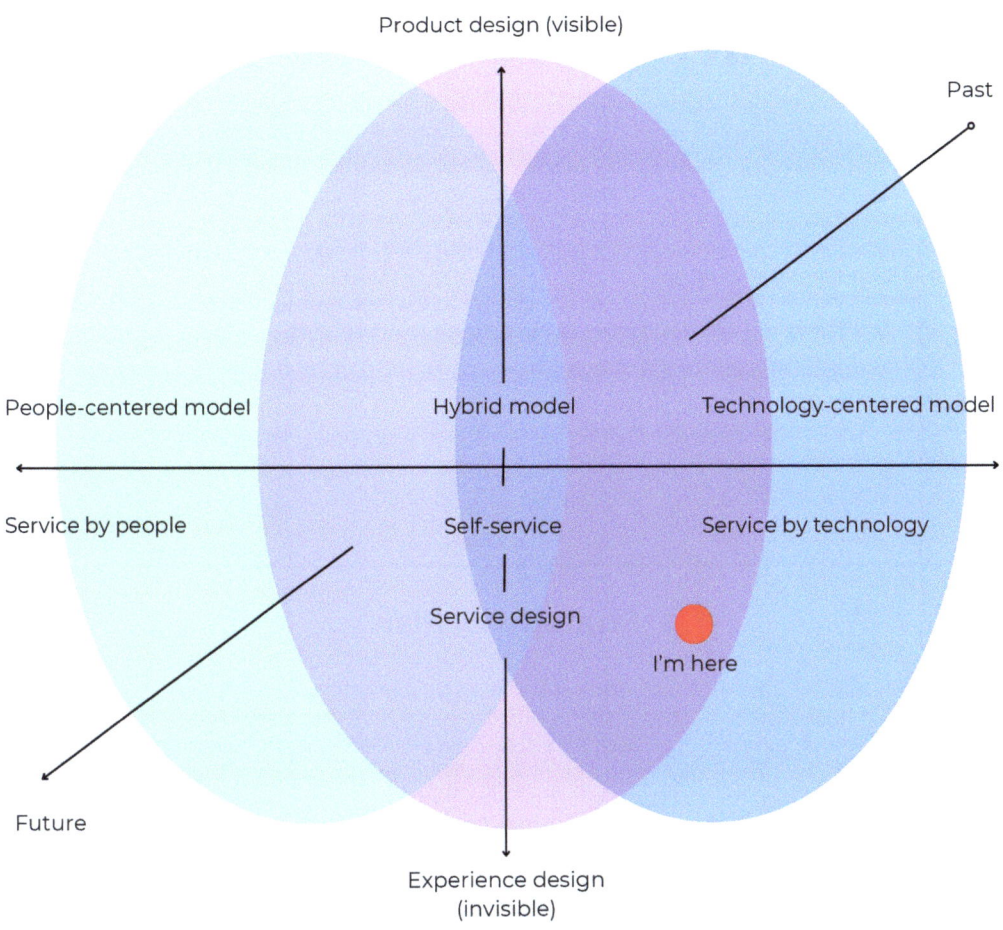

Product design (visible)

Past

People-centered model · Hybrid model · Technology-centered model

Service by people · Self-service · Service by technology

Service design

I'm here

Future

Experience design
(invisible)

Modified from Lee S., Yang M. C., de Weck O. L., Lee C., Coughlin J. F., et al. (2023). Macro-trend study under service system: Preliminary research in service innovation and engineering technology. In: Umar Zakir Abdul Hamid, & Mari Suoheimo (eds.). Service Design for Emerging Technologies Product Development: Bridging the Interdisciplinary Knowledge Gap, pp. 45–72. Springer.

Service design tools for strategy

"Thinking like a designer can transform the way you develop products, services, processes – and even strategy"

Tim Brown, 2008
Harvard Business review

As a product manager, you might be responsible for or involved in the preparation of:

- a product strategy
- a business strategy
- a brand strategy
- a go-to-market strategy
- an innovation strategy

Strategy vs. Plan

"*Plans typically have to do with the resources you're going to spend. Those are more comfortable because you control them. A strategy, on the other hand, specifies a competitive outcome that you wish to achieve, which involves customers wanting your product or service. The tricky thing about that is that you don't control them.*"

Roger Martin: A Plan Is Not a Strategy, Harvard Business Review on YouTube, June 2022

For example...

The author's **strategy** for increasing user involvement in medical devices is to create awareness of service design. She also took a strategic decision to approach the field through product management (bottom-up). There is some level of uncertainty in this chosen strategy. The future shows if it was a winning strategy or not.

The author's **plan** to execute the strategy was to write a service design handbook for medical device product management. She also needed to plan the launch and marketing activities to support awareness about the book.

Service design tools for strategy and sustainability

Here are some examples of service design tools for strategy. Templates online often include an excellent explanation of the purpose of the tool and instructions for use.

The VMSV Pyramid (Vision, Mission, Strategies and Values) is a great tool for discussion, co-creation, and building understanding.
The 5 Bold Steps Vision Canvas by David Sibbet helps identify the things that support and challenge your vision and build the steps towards it.
The Strategy Explorer by Dr. Stefan Pastuszka takes the classic SWOT analysis to a strategic level.
The stakeholder map, ecosystem map, value map, actors map, and ecology map (Smaply, Mural, Miro, servicedesigntools.org etc.) clarify the stakeholders and the relationship between parties.

Service design is a quickly evolving field, and service design tools and design thinking are also used for environmental and sustainability purposes. Here are some of the **tools that help concretize or discover opportunities related to circular economy.**

Circularity Deck by Jan Konietzko is a tool for discovering opportunities for circular business in an intuitive and accessible way. Based on Konietzko's PhD work, it helps organizations get started in their sustainability transformation. Circularitydeck.com provides a video for quick learning.
The Circular Canvas and The Value Chain Canvas by Circulab allow you to break down your projects to design more sustainable solutions.
The Circular Value Chain Tool by Danish Design Center (DDC) helps you reflect, discuss, and investigate opportunities to create circular loops around your specific product.

Fascinated about different design disciplines?

Could life-centric business models, life-centered design, futures design, planet-centered design, or non-human personas bring opportunities to reach your professional objectives?

We tend to stick to familiar thought paths. Learning new ways of thinking and approaching problems can be a great source of creativity.

What's different when your medical device is software?

Managing a medical device that's software is a different ball game. While the same regulations apply, software offers unique opportunities and challenges.

What's different about software?
- New possibilities: With software, you can continuously develop and improve the product. This enables faster updates and changes based on user feedback.
- Ongoing involvement: As a product manager, you'll need to remain actively engaged. Regular monitoring, refinement, and ensuring compliance will be key responsibilities.

Why use service design?
Service design provides tools to ensure your software remains safe, user-friendly, and compliant with regulations throughout its lifecycle.

How to use service design during market surveillance

- **Enhance user experience:** Service design helps identify and address usability issues while adapting the product to meet changing user needs. Real-world feedback, structured through service design, allows for targeted and effective improvements.
- **Ensure compliance:** Service design supports compliance with frameworks like MDR and IEC 62366-1. An iterative approach ensures the software meets user-centered design standards and regulatory requirements.
- **Manage risks:** Risk-prone areas can be identified early through user pathway mapping and service design workshops. This proactive approach helps mitigate hazards caused by usage errors, ensuring the product remains safe and reliable.

Implementing service design: the practical approach

Incorporate design reviews:
Design Input Reviews (DIRs) and Design Output Reviews (DORs) are essential elements of a robust development process. These reviews provide a forum for communicating findings from user feedback and service design analysis, ensuring that needs are translated into actionable plans. They also facilitate collaboration between product managers and development teams, enabling efficient and effective decision-making.

by Antti Brunni

Facilitate cross-team communication:
Product management processes should foster seamless communication between the development team and product managers. Depending on the management structure, these processes can integrate service design insights through structured reviews and iterative feedback cycles. This allows user needs, risks, and development priorities to be systematically addressed and aligned.

Address reluctance for user testing:
Development teams may be hesitant to expose prototypes to user testing. However, service design and co-creation methods can still provide valuable insights during early stages, enabling the identification and elimination of potential risks before they escalate. This approach reduces the likelihood of costly rework or delays later in the product lifecycle.

Document systematically:
Service design methods, such as co-design workshops and iterative evaluations, should be used to generate comprehensive documentation. This ensures that all findings, design changes, and risk management decisions are recorded to meet regulatory requirements effectively.

Applying service design across development stages

Service design can be utilized at every phase of software development, from establishing a need and task analysis to conceptual design, detailed design, implementation, and use. Integrating service design tools ensures that each stage aligns with user needs, minimizes risks, and maintains compliance, contributing to a smoother, more efficient development process.

By embedding service design into your product management workflow, you can enhance collaboration, improve product safety, and achieve a balance between usability and regulatory compliance.

1. Ogrodnik, P. (2013). Medical Device Design: Innovation from Concept to Market. Elsevier.
2. Granlund, T. (2020). RegOps – diving into the dilemma of agile software development in regulated industry. Solita.
3. Cross, N. (2006). Designerly ways of knowing. In: Cross, N. (ed.). Designerly Ways of Knowing, pp. 1–13. Springer.
4. Gericke, K., & Blessing, L. (2012). An analysis of design process models across disciplines. 12th International Design Conference – DESIGN 2012.
5. Hohm, A., Happel, O., Hurtienne, J., & Grundgeiger, T. (2022). User experience in safety critical domains: a survey on motivational orientations and psychological need satisfaction in acute care. Cognition, Technology & Work, 24(2), 247–260.
6. Savioja, P., Liinasuo, M., & Koskinen, H. (2014). User experience: does it matter in complex systems? Cognition, Technology & Work, 16(4), 429–449.

Part IV

Service Design for Medical Device Manufacturer

Adopting service design in an organization

The aim of this handbook is to increase **knowledge about service design among medical device manufacturers to better involve the users and other stakeholders.** The perspective is bottom-up and the focus is on product management. While medical device product managers can naturally use service design without the acceptance of top management, top level support is essential to achieve the full potential of service design and to adopt it in the culture of the organization. This is why I've dedicated a chapter to the leaders in medical device manufacturing organizations.

The benefits of service design for an organization may include (1, 2, 3)
- increased user and patient satisfaction and safety
- harmonization of services and user experience
- less time, miles, and money spent on product training
- attraction and retention of a new generation of talents
- deep exploration of competitive advantages and market demand
- transition from innovation to creating value for profitability
- a way to dispel silos and barriers between departments
- a great positive financial impact.

Kretzschmar (3) surveyed a large amount of data from different-sized Danish companies to understand the economic effects of design and demonstrated a correlation between the use of design and the company's success. The growth in gross revenues was almost **22% higher for companies that employed design** compared to companies in general (n=841 companies).

How to adopt service design in an organization

Taking on the service design process, tools, and thinking requires active learning over time. According to Mahmoud-Jouini (4), if a tech company is motivated, there are a few different ways to make design thinking part of the company's culture:
- Some companies have trained a big group of employees in design thinking (e.g. Infosys).
- Some have hired designers and had them collaborate with engineers (e.g. IBM).
- Some have created a category of employees whose role it is to spread design thinking in the organization as "innovation catalysts" or service design ambassadors (e.g. Intuit).
- Some have acquired design companies to bring in design thinking skills (McKinsey acquired Luna, while Accenture acquired Fjord).

Korpikoski & Miettinen (5) studied the ways service design as an in-house methodology supports the enhancement of human-centricity in an expert-driven organization. They found out that experiential learning is key when changing formerly technology-oriented, expert-driven attitudes. After acquiring practical experience in service design, experts talked about a 'eureka moment' when they realized the deep meaning of human-centricity. They mentioned **learning to 'leave the expertise' and thus becoming humbler and improving their ability to listen to the customer.**

Anyone can learn service design. That said, **service design cannot be learned solely from books.** It requires action and experiential practice. Having a strategy for adopting service design on operational and cultural levels makes it easier for members of the organization to take action. The strategy can be built with the input of an in-house service designer or an external consultant. The following pages discuss models of evaluating the **design maturity** of an organization. The design ladder described on page 42 can be useful when creating a design adoption strategy. This chapter ends with a practical approach to the burning question of the **cost of service design for an organization.**

> "If you think good design is expensive, you should look at the cost of bad design"
>
> Ralf Speth, CEO of Jaguar

Organizational transformation through service design

Krista Korpikoski's doctoral thesis (6) brings up several important aspects to consider when adopting service design in an organization through a case study of a corporation with a long history in engineering and manufacturing. The main research question of the thesis is: What is required for an organization, to transform its working culture towards human-and customer-centricity, in order to enable the efficient integration of in-house service design?

1. Hamid, U. Z. A., & Suoheimo, M. (2023). Product development challenges for emerging technologies and service design roles in addressing the issues. In: Umar Zakir Abdul Hamid, & Mari Suoheimo (eds.). Service Design for Emerging Technologies Product Development: Bridging the Interdisciplinary Knowledge Gap, pp. 9–22. Springer.
2. Korper, A. K., Patrício, L., Holmlid, S., & Witell, L. (2020). Service design as an innovation approach in technology startups: A longitudinal multiple case study. Creativity and Innovation Management, 29(2), 303–323.
3. Kretzschmar, A. (2003). The Economic Effects of Design. National Agency for Enterprise and Housing.
4. Mahmoud-Jouini, S. B., Fixson, S. K., & Boulet, D. (2019). Making design thinking work: Adapting an innovation approach to fit a large technology-driven firm. Research Technology Management, 62(5), 50–58.
5. Korpikoski K., & Miettinen S. (2023). Organizational transformation through in-house service design: A case study of a multinational manufacturing corporation. In: Umar Zakir Abdul Hamid, & Mari Suoheimo (eds.). Service Design for Emerging Technologies Product Development: Bridging the Interdisciplinary Knowledge Gap, pp. 163–182. Springer.
6. Korpikoski, K. (2023). Organizational transformation through service design: The journey towards human- and customer-centricity. Doctoral dissertation, University of Lapland.

The design maturity of an organization

The first Design Ladder (1) framework was developed to assess the financial impact of design within organizations.
Additionally, the Design Ladder serves as a tool for evaluating an organization's design maturity and for planning actions and operations that foster the advancement of design capabilities.

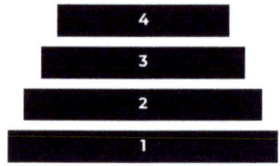

Step No. 1 No design:
Design is an inconspicuous part of, for instance, product development and performed by members of staff, who are not design professionals. Design solutions are based on the perception of functionality and aesthetics shared by the people involved. The points of view of end-users play very little or no part at all.

Step No. 2 Design as styling:
Design is perceived as a final aesthetic finish of a product. In some cases, professional designers may perform the task, but generally other professions are involved.

Step No. 3 Design as process:
Design is not a finite part of a process but a work method adopted very early in product development. The design solution is adapted to the task and focused on the end-user and requires a multidisciplinary approach, e.g. involving process technicians, material technologists, marketing and organisational people.

Step No. 4 Design as innovation:
The designer collaborates with the owner/management in adopting an innovative approach to all – or substantial parts – of the business foundation. The design process combined with the company vision and future role in the value chain are important elements.

New versions of the model have emerged since its first appearance (the steps described above). For example, **Doherty et al.** (2) suggested adding a cultural aspect to support the operational aspect of design maturity development, while **The Service Design Maturity Model by The Service Design Network** (3) described five stages of maturity: Explore, Prove, Scale, Integrate, and Thrive.

Design Maturity Matrix

The dmi:Design Maturity Matrix is a simple mapping tool for measuring the maturity of design in an organization. It can be used to
- understand the process maturity of the design organization
- create a common language for strategic discussions with cross-functional peers
- align investments in design with business strategy.

Download a free template at dmi.org.

The voice of the designers and the design utilizer

For their Design Maturity Survey Report 2024 (5), Ornamo Ry asked 35 designers in different industries in Finland for their views on **how design creates value for the organization**. Most of them worked as in-house designers in the private sector. Their top four answers were:

1) we achieve more user-friendly products
2) we enhance the company's brand
3) we experience increased customer satisfaction
4) we develop new solutions and business areas.

Finnish technology company Vaisala, on the other hand, was awarded the 2024 Ornamo Award (5) as a design utilizer. This is how Vaisala's Design Director Sauli Laitinen summarized their approach:

"We don't follow the tradition of star designers, where a designer shows up and performs miracles. Our work is more about helping others. We use design methods to help understand who the users of our products are, where and why they use them."

1. Kretzschmar, A. (2003). The Economic Effects of Design. National Agency for Enterprise and Housing.
2. Doherty, R., Wrigley, C., Matthews, J., & Bucolo, S. (2015). Climbing the design ladder: Step by step. Revista D: Design, Educação, Sociedade e Sustentabilidade, 7(1), 60–82.
3. Corsten, N., & Prick, J. (2020). The service design maturity model: A strategic framework to embed service design into an organisation. Touchpoint, 12(1).
4. Design Management Institute, dmi.org
5. Ornamo Ry (2024). Design Maturity survey report.

How much does service design cost?

Implementing service design, like any other effort to maintain or increase an organization's competitiveness, is an investment. Before discussing the cost of service design, we need to define the currency. Are we talking about euros, dollars, CO2 compensation, patents, or trademarks? All of these can be relevant assets when it comes to medical device business finance. Service design doesn't provide quick wins, so to only focus on a short-term increase in gross margin is not a fair way to evaluate its return on investment.

This chapter may help you evaluate whether or not to invest on service design. After estimating the amount of money an individual or organization needs to invest in service design, we can compare the investment with potential benefits.

Individual level (€)

The investment of time required to learn the basics of service design varies from a couple of weeks to a couple of months. Course prizes may be anything between zero (public universities) and €4000 (academic and commercial providers). With basic knowledge, a product manager can improve their work efficiency and act as a design enabler. Service design is learned by doing, and the skill level acquired depends on the amount of practice. A couple of weeks of intensive practical learning can give a product manager a more human-centered way of thinking and improve their user research skills and efficiency. **To become a professional service designer takes years.**

Organizational level (€)

Depending on where you are, an external service designer could cost you €500–1500 per day, while the salary of an in-house service designer would be €2000–7000 per month. The time it takes to see an impact depends on your organization's size and level of motivation. For a start-up, that time could be 11 months (1), while in a multinational corporation, it could even take four years to see significant signs of transformation (2).

Once you have a clear picture of what's needed, you may have to justify the investment in service design. For that, you need to
- reflect on your objectives (strategy and vision)
- evaluate what you might get in return (how increased human-centricity impacts your business).

Return on investment

It's debatable whether traditional ROI calculations apply to innovation businesses (3). The benefits of service design for the organization can be divided into short-term and long-term effects. KPIs are a good way to evaluate short-term performance and the impact of an investment. Good KPIs for innovation are related to innovation initiatives, processes, and outcomes.

Conversely, ROI is a long-term metric. One way to demonstrate the reasoning behind investing in service design is presenting a straightforward business case that accounts for costs, benefits, and risks. For a deeper understanding, you could contemplate two scenarios with different timeframes, for example:
Case 1: the impact after year one
Case 2: the impact of climbing the design maturity ladder from "no design" to "design as process".

The following table suggests some aspects you may want to consider in your business case.

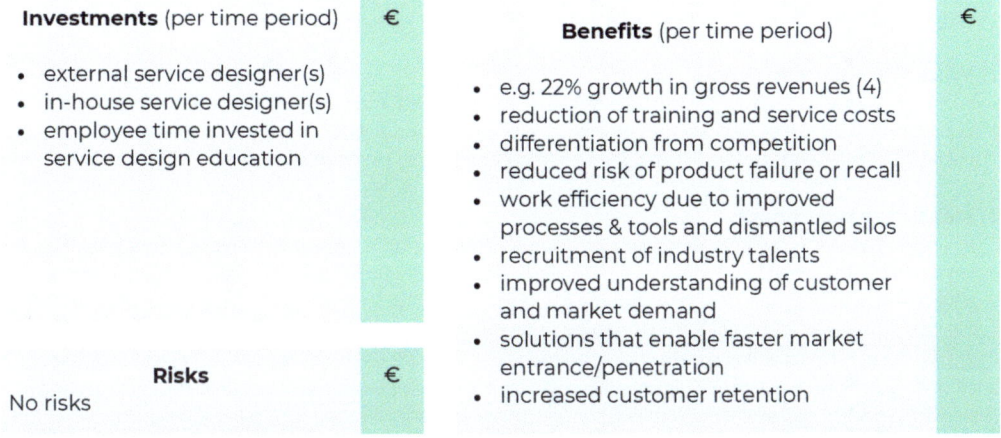

Investments (per time period)	€	Benefits (per time period)	€
• external service designer(s) • in-house service designer(s) • employee time invested in service design education		• e.g. 22% growth in gross revenues (4) • reduction of training and service costs • differentiation from competition • reduced risk of product failure or recall • work efficiency due to improved processes & tools and dismantled silos • recruitment of industry talents • improved understanding of customer and market demand • solutions that enable faster market entrance/penetration • increased customer retention	
Risks	€		
No risks			

Impact beyond the organization

A holistic approach to designing services and products can have a great impact on healthcare systems and global sustainability targets. Many health issues are systemic challenges, and a shared effort of companies and societies can result in innovative services and infrastructural investments with positive outcomes for both health and the environment.

Especially if your strategy and vision include aspects of sustainability, you may want to include the potential of sustainability design in your business case.

As mentioned in the beginning of this handbook, user involvement can have a widespread impact on patients' and caregivers' lives and the resources of healthcare organizations. If this is relevant to your values, vision and strategy, it may be something to highlight in your business case.

Measuring the impact of a single project

Setting project-specific metrics is another way to understand the impact of service design. There is no one-size-fits-all way to measure the impact of service design on a project level; instead, you need to evaluate what's important to you. The metrics also depend on whether you are creating something new or improving an existing product/service. These basic steps and the following example may give you some inspiration.

1) First, define your customer(s).
2) Ask what your customer wants.
3) Finally, define what to measure.

A good metric is SMART: Specific, Measurable, Achievable, Relevant, and Time-bound.

Example

This example is inspired by an IDEO case "A More Comfortable Pap Smear" (5).

1) Customers:
- a woman conducting new self-sampling for cervical cancer screening
- a gynecologist conducting cervical cancer screening procedure

2) What the customer wants:
A quick and easy sampling procedure and intuitive results. A device that is safe for home use and provides a comfortable and ergonomic user experience. Additionally, the device must be compatible with laboratories' standard sample processing procedures.

3) Measuring the impact:
Customer: The new device saves the patient's and physician's time (minutes) and money (€) compared to the previous procedure. FTE (Full-Time Equivalent) can be used to measure the workload of both parties. The new device also improves the sampling experience and screening adherence, measured by NPS (net promoter score).
Manufacturer: The user experience can be measured by an ease-of-use rating, returning users, NPS (net promoter score), CES (customer effort score), user mistakes/incident reporting, metrics related to market expansion, financial metrics, etc.
Society: The device increases the accessibility of screening and patients' willingness to participate (number of annual screenings). This has a long-term financial and health-related impact on the patient and reduces the use of healthcare resources (€, time).

1. Korper, A. K., Patrício, L., Holmlid, S., & Witell, L. (2020). Service design as an innovation approach in technology startups: A longitudinal multiple case study. Creativity and Innovation Management, 29(2), 303–323.
2. Korpikoski K., & Miettinen S. (2023) Organizational transformation through in-house service design: A case study of a multinational manufacturing corporation. In: Umar Zakir Abdul Hamid, & Mari Suoheimo (eds.). Service Design for Emerging Technologies Product Development: Bridging the Interdisciplinary Knowledge Gap, pp. 163–182. Springer.
3. Strategyzer.com (2024). How to measure ROI for innovation – your complete guide.
4. Kretzschmar, A. (2003). The Economic Effects of Design. National Agency for Enterprise and Housing.
5. IDEO.com. A more comfortable Pap smear. Available at https://www.ideo.com/works/teal-health.

Part V

How to Do
Service Design

Process phases step by step

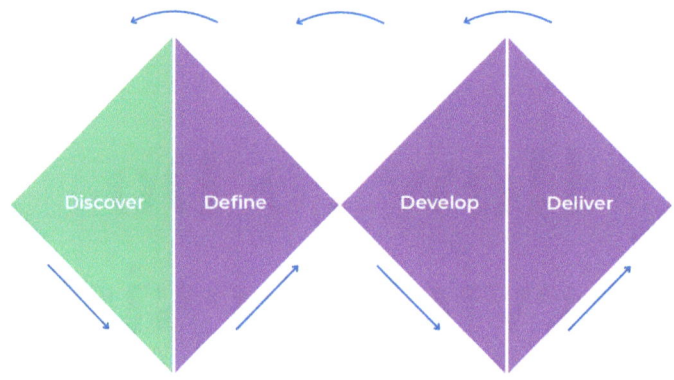

Discover

Discover, research, understand, empathize

Right, let's get brainstorming and generate new ideas! Oh, wait. Before innovating and ideating, we have an entire diamond to complete: the diamond of discovery and definition. The service design process doesn't start with ideating. A well-completed first diamond is the ticket to the root of the problem. After the first diamond, we should be confident that we are solving the right problem. To define the problem statement, we need to have deep understanding of the current situation.

During the first half of the diamond, we use divergent thinking, i.e. collect different types of information. We might even collect data that's irrelevant to the actual problem. Why? Because we don't know the problem yet. The divergent, opening phases of the diamonds may be the most difficult parts of the service design process, as we easily assume we already know what's relevant to solving the problem. The key is to not jump to conclusions too early on. You may have ideas about how to solve the problem, but you should save them for later. For now, focus on empathy and understanding the users and the environment. Resolution is comforting and satisfying for the human mind, but if we try to reach it too early in the process, important facts or ideas might remain undiscovered. This is something we want to avoid.

In this phase, you should
- generate data
- gain understanding about the problem, the ecosystem, and the culture
- develop empathy towards the users by learning about their pains, gains, challenges, reasons to engage, relationships, etc.

Tools and methods for achieving this
- interview
- observation
- cultural probes
- storyboard
- market research
- benchmarking
- ethnography, video ethnography (check out Indeemo)

Explore qualitative user research techniques

- Interview questions, interview techniques
- Data triangulation (e.g. interview, survey, observation)
- How to practice active listening
- How to set qualitative and quantitative metrics
- Generative, formative and summative research methods

Observation

Not all essential information is or can be verbalized. The customer may not be allowed to say certain things out loud, they might feel embarrassed, or they could forget about something. Observation can reveal hidden aspects of your customer's behavior. Observation can be structured or unstructured, participative, recorded, unrecorded, covert, overt, or done through shadowing. Just like with any other research technique, it's important to document your observations. Observation combined with interviews might reveal silent aspects such as the feelings, dreams, values, or experiences of your customer.

Interview

As Rob Fitzpatrick explains in his book **The Mom Test** (2013), there are good and bad questions and it's not the interviewees' responsibility to tell you the truth. Explore different interview techniques: structured, non-structured, semi-structured, focus group, in-depth, narrative, and expert interviews. Choose a technique that fits your purpose. Instead of inviting the interviewees to your office, meet them in their natural environment (where the device is used).

"Checklist for a snappy researcher"
from **Ethnography Fieldguide** by **SITRA**

☐ Always listen more than you speak.

☐ Remember that it is your responsibility to be true for the thoughts, behaviors and expressions of people you are studying.

☐ Conduct the research in the natural context of the topic you are studying, and try to create a fun and welcoming atmosphere, if appropriate.

☐ Start the interview with a general description of the goal of the study, but don't provide a too narrow focus as that might limit the responses you will get.

☐ Encourage people to share their thoughts and go about their business freely, while you follow along.

☐ Avoid leading questions and questions that can be answered with only yes/no answers. Ask follow up questions.

☐ Prepare an outline of the interview questions you would like to ask beforehand, but don't be afraid to stray from it.

☐ Be a shutterbug and snap photos of interesting things and behaviors.

☐ Keep your ears and eyes open also after the recorder stops, this is often the moment when you get valuable revelations.

Cultural probe
A cultural probe can be a set of tasks the user performs to provide data for the designer or product manager. It's one way to collect empirical data and an excellent method to support observation and interviews.

Example: A (medical device) robot that assists elderly patients in living at home and allows them to remotely communicate with caregivers.
The aim is to study the cultural context of the user at home to understand aspects that may impact the usability or safety of the product. This may also reveal new service and business opportunities.

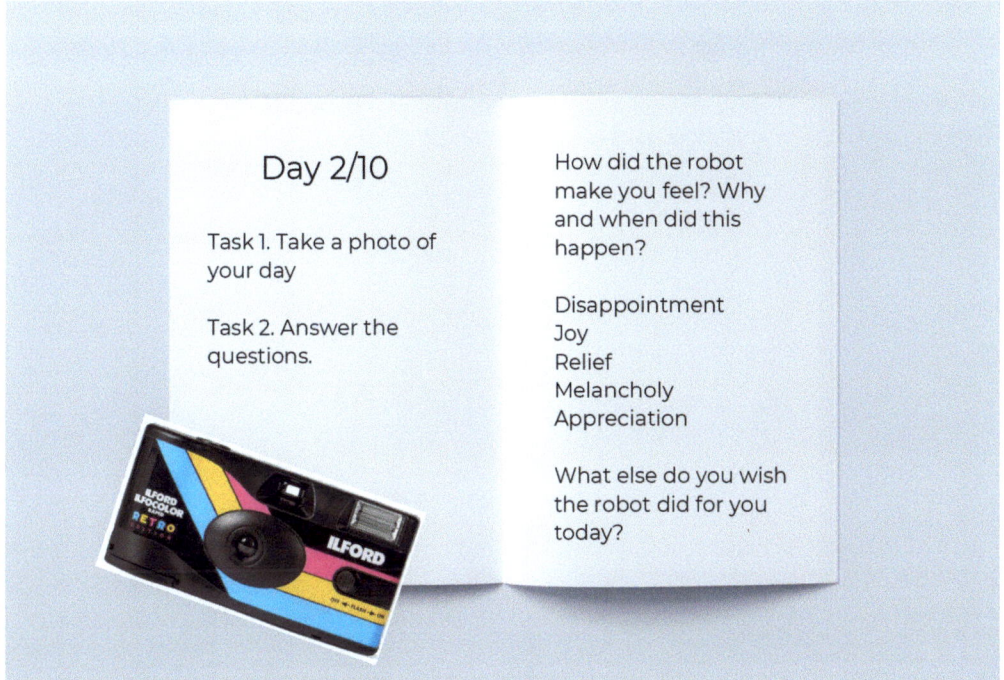

Determining **research questions** helps you plan interview questions, observation, or probes. A good question is focused and researchable. Instead of asking "How to improve geriatric care?" you could ask, for example:

"Which factors influence the adoption of wearable health devices among older adults?"
or
"How does the use of mobile health apps influence medication adherence among diabetes patients?"

Setting a clear focus will help you in the next phase as you start analyzing and crystallizing the research data.

2+3=23

Your reality is not the same as the customer's reality,
so listen carefully.

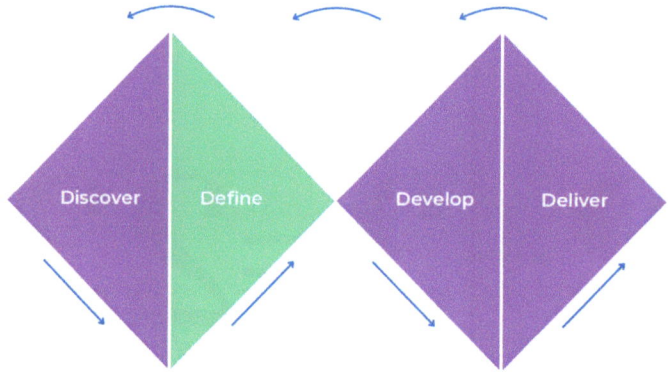

Define

Define, identify, converge, concept, specify

In the definition phase, you do what it takes to define the correct problem statement to start generating ideas for. The data you've collected will now be analyzed and converged using the tools mentioned below. Patterns and themes will be summarized in text, images, charts, or another suitable format that serves the next phase, ideation. It can be challenging to summarize, analyze, and find the essence of all the data, but remember this: you do not work alone, and in this phase, you can always iterate and go back to ask the user.

In this phase, you should
- use human-centered methods to find the essence of the data you've gathered
- use the collected data to define the root cause of the problem
- hold your horses, avoid jumping into conclusions. Put your ideas in the parking lot – they will be useful in the next phase!

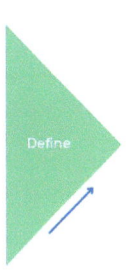

Tools and methods for achieving this
- user personas
- empathy map
- user/customer journey map
- service blueprint
- stakeholder map
- gigamap
- How Might We (HMW)
- Day in the Life
- storyboard
- bull's eye diagram
- current state analysis
- 5 whys

When explaining the user type to the development team, the product manager needs to be specific but keep it concise. Instead of expecting the team to know the role and responsibilities of, for example, a lab technician, the product manager can explain them by using a customer persona, a customer journey map, or even a storyboard. Brief but detailed user descriptions that include the user's emotions (such as stress caused by time pressure, or safety concerns) combined with a time-based visualization of the user's main touchpoints will make the developers' life easier. To understand what your internal customers need to successfully execute their work, you can utilize the same empathizing methods you used with external customers.

User persona, customer persona

Any product development project starts with defining the user(s). The user persona is a service design tool that helps identify and illustrate the product's current and/or potential user archetypes. It's a tool for analysis, communication, and ideation, and essential for many other tools such as the customer journey map, How Might We, empathy map, and service blueprint. It serves a purpose in many different parts of the service design process; for example, a user persona can act as a boundary object to align an interdisciplinary team (1), or it can be used to summarize and share research findings. A user persona typically includes a brief description of the persona, their experience, pains, and gains. It may also incorporate relevant numerical information such as "70% of their patients are women". All the information should be based on real data.

How do you determine the appropriate number of personas?
The number of personas you need depends on the project and the service/product. Medical device products often have users or customers on multiple levels. Preparing personas can be a part of your research analysis; you can start with 10–20 personas and filter them further to end up with 2–8 archetypes. Keeping a high number of persona profiles on board across the project is challenging. It's better to choose as few as you can without compromising the data. Your business/product strategy may also help you select the key personas.

Example
The prototype of this handbook was designed based on interviews of eight professionals. The data was distilled into two personas (see the next page):

- Pete, the 'minimum viable persona', represents the baseline user whose needs the author aims to meet at a minimum.
- Diana, the director, has distinct needs and challenges. Her perspective must be considered, too, but her needs are taken into account if they do not clash with Pete's.

1. Stickdorn, M., Hormess, M. E., Lawrence, A., & Schneider, J. (2018). This Is Service Design Doing. O'Reilly Media, Inc.

Pete, Product Manager (Company Y)

How can we turn product-related problems into features to our benefit?

Brief description
Pete has a couple of years of experience in product management. He is self-taught, with no role-specific onboarding back when he started. His senior colleagues seem to have a fixed way of working, and their young colleagues follow suit. Pete is in survival mode and has no time for learning.

Main job
Pete's main job is to deliver the VOC to R&D and ensure product safety; however, due to the structure of the organization, the account manager has more time with the customer than the product manager. Customer feedback often comes in as second-hand information. Pete needs to understand the core reasons for the customers' problems and requests and communicate them to the R&D department. His challenging tasks include designing user interview questions and creating user requirements/specifications. He often feels like a lonely rider with a lot of responsibility but limited power.

Personality
Pete is a positive person, and customers like him. He likes to travel to meet customers and train them. He has great communication skills.

Customers
R&D, sales, regulatory, production, finance, distributors, users, procurement (the customers'), heads of lab etc.

Service design experience
No experience, hasn't heard about it. Pete is detail-oriented, and the idea of quick prototypes sounds terrifying to him.

Gains
- Customer satisfaction is relatively high
- Pete has gained a senior position in the company

Pains
- User requirements and product specifications in an international market
- Searching for new tricks to create cash flow

Diana, Director, Product Management (Company X)

"It's not a new idea to base development on the voice of the customer,
but it's great to have a process for that."

Brief description
Diana is an experienced human and product manager. She's hard-working and travels frequently. She doesn't use service design, hasn't heard about it before. "I'm an old dog."

Main job
Diana's main job is to keep employees happy and motivated and their skills up to date. Financial goals set by the management and board guide her work, and she often needs to make difficult decisions. It's her responsibility to design and update the product portfolio together with the team. She understands the market well and acts as a strong link between the management of different departments, especially R&D and sales/marketing.

Personality
Diana is an empathetic person who can see the bigger picture. She is a little attached to the old ways that have been proven to work well. She likes to think she is open-minded. Her communication skills are great.

Customers
Product managers, management, board, investors

Reason to engage
- Diana would like to learn about service design but thinks that it's impossible to integrate it to the company culture alone.
- Tools for convincing the rest of the management about the financial benefits of service design

Pains
"We've have bad experiences talking about new products to the customer too early on. Product development is such a long process. Building expectations with the customer and sales team and then making them wait for the product for years creates dissatisfaction."

Gains
Diana feels that she has understood the importance of emotions in decision making and recognizes that we tend to forget it in product development.

Customer journey map

A customer journey map is a visual timeline that documents a sequence of service engagements and interactions. (1) It may help, for example, explore potential solutions (2), generate ideas, or manage risks. Discover customer journey map templates on **Miro** and **Mural**.

The basic building blocks of user journey mapping (3):
1. actor
2. scenario + expectations
3. journey phases
4. actions, mindsets, and emotions
5. opportunities

Example

Customer persona: "Susanne from the lab"

Scenario: Susanne is ordering DxFirm's consumables for the first time.

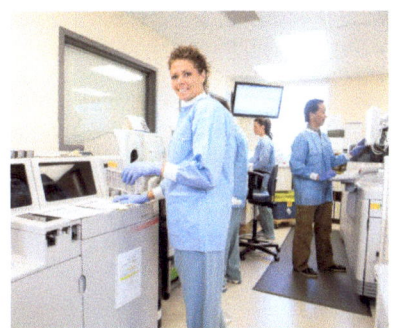

	Before ordering		Ordering				After ordering	
Action	Notification from DxFirm	Checks inventory and exp dates	Enters lab system	Drafts an order	Verification from supervisor	Places an order	Thank you for your order	Delivery, unpacking
Touch-point	Device	Fridge/Storage/Device	Lab system	Lab system	Lab system	DxFirm's website	Email	Lab
Emotion	😊	😲	😕	😕	😕	😊	😊	😄
Feels/thinks	"It's great to be notified when it's time to order"	"It's time-consuming to walk back and forth"	"Where can I find the product codes and package sizes?"	"I hope I didn't make any typos"	"Now, where do I place the order?"	"There's not much data I need to fill in manually"	"I hope the critical consumables arrive fast"	"Great, they arrived quickly and in good condition!"
Opportu-nities	-	Automatize the list of exp dates?	Reduce manual work	Reduce manual work	Guidance	Further reduce manual work?	Inform: estimate of the delivery time	-

1. Penin, L. 2018. An Introduction to Service Design: Designing the Invisible. Bloomsbury Visual Arts.
2. Stickdorn, M., Hormess, M. E., Lawrence, A., & Schneider, J. (2018). This Is Service Design Doing. O'Reilly Media, Inc.
3. Gibbons, S. (2018). Journey Mapping 101. NN Group.

Value creation

It's a no-brainer that to achieve successful business, we need to understand our customers. But what do we need to know about them? What's essential is the information that helps us understand the customer as a human being influenced by the people, culture, and history around them. That allows us to grasp the process of value creation. **And why do we talk about value creation?** Because that's where the next opportunity for a business, service, or product innovation could be hiding. Even when it doesn't directly lead to a groundbreaking innovation, understanding how and where value is created can help us determine if our offering is viable in the current market. It may also guide us in designing a solution that outperforms competitors within its category.

The story of Henry Ford? Again? Yes. The famous Mr. Ford invented the automobile even though customers asked for faster horses. Someone could say he was clever for not listening to what the customers said but doing what he thought was right. We could also say he was clever because he understood the value of transportation to the customers at that time and in that environment. He identified the correct problem and was able to fix it with new technology. Customer value formation remains a key challenge for marketing theorists even with extensive research on both B2C and B2B settings. In 1995, Gummesson argued that the traditional division between goods and services is long outdated. Customers do not buy goods or services; they buy offerings that render services that create value. The following picture, although radically simplified, illustrates how the view of customer value creation has evolved on a theoretical level. The original process picture by Grönroos and Gummerus (2014) may be inspirational if innovation trough product and service value creation is of your interest.

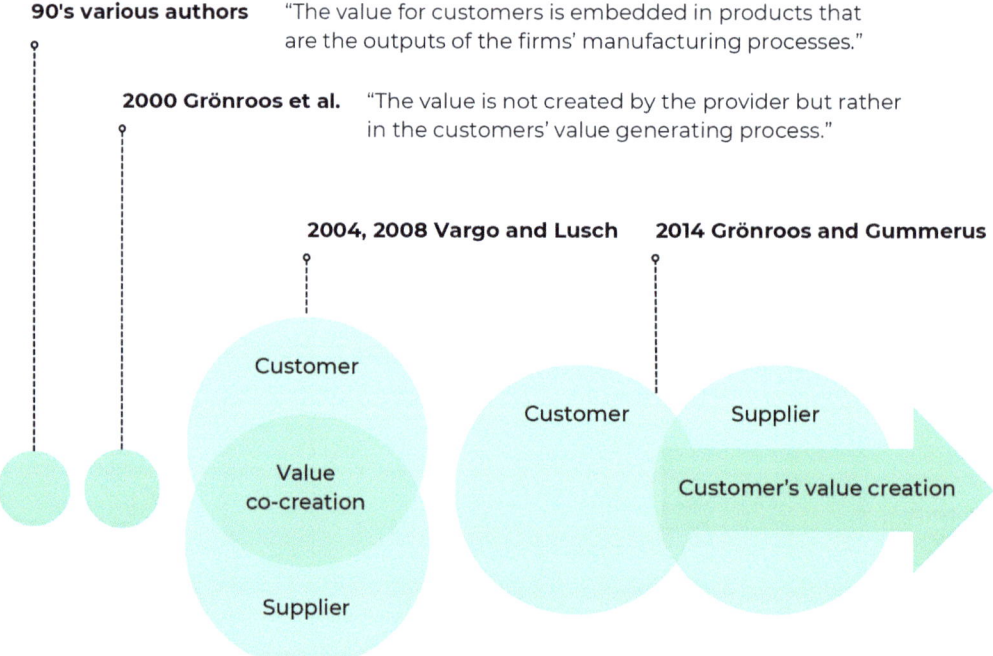

90's various authors "The value for customers is embedded in products that are the outputs of the firms' manufacturing processes."

2000 Grönroos et al. "The value is not created by the provider but rather in the customers' value generating process."

2004, 2008 Vargo and Lusch   **2014 Grönroos and Gummerus**

Customer

Value co-creation

Supplier

Customer   Supplier

Customer's value creation

In the case of a medical device manufacturer, one product can have customers or users on several levels, which can make the value generating process very complex. Let's take a simplified example: the manufacturer produces a diagnostic device that is used by laboratory representatives, but the result it gives – the actual value – is consumed by a doctor who will use it for the wellbeing of the real end user, the patient. For each customer, the value is different. The device manufacturer may have very little interaction with some of the customer levels, but they still create value together for all levels. A big part of value creation occurs outside the visibility of the manufacturer, and it may be unexpected or hard to observe. (3)

These tools may further clarify value creation and relationships between stakeholders:
- empathy map
- Value Proposition Canvas by Alex Osterwalder (Strategyzer)
- value chain map (Smaply and various other sources)
- Business Model Canvas by Alexander Osterwalder & Yves Pigneur
- Strategy Explorer by Stefan Patuszka
- stakeholder mapping by Somersault Innovation or LUMA Institute

To wrap up this chapter, here's an excellent quote about customer value from famous academics in the field of experience economy, Pine and Gilmore (6). To highlight the fact that medical devices are not just goods, I modified this smart quote to fit the world of medical devices.

"Services are about time well saved while experiences are about time well spent."

Pine & Gilmore 2019

Modification:
"Services are about patient safety, while experiences are about the sense of caring."

Koho 2025

1. Gummesson, E. (1995). Relationship marketing: Its role in the service economy. Understanding Services Management, 244, 68.
2. Grönroos, C. (2008). Service logic revisited: Who creates value? And who co-creates? European Business Review, 20(4), 298–314.
3. Strandvik, T., Heinonen, K., & Vollmer, S. (2019). Revealing business customers' hidden value formation in service. The Journal of Business & Industrial Marketing, 34(6), 1145–1159.
4. Pencarelli, T. (2017). Marketing in an experiential perspective: Toward the Experience Logic. Mercati e Competitività, 2, 7–14.
5. Grönroos, C., & Gummerus, J. (2014). The service revolution and its marketing implications: Service logic vs service-dominant logic. Managing Service Quality, 24(3), 206–229.
6. Pine II, B. J., & Gilmore, J. H. (2019). Preview + Welcome to the experience economy. In: B. Joseph Pine II, & James H. Gilmore (eds.). The Experience Economy: Competing for Customer Time, Attention, and Money (revised edition), pp. ix–xxx + 1–34. Harvard Business Review Press.

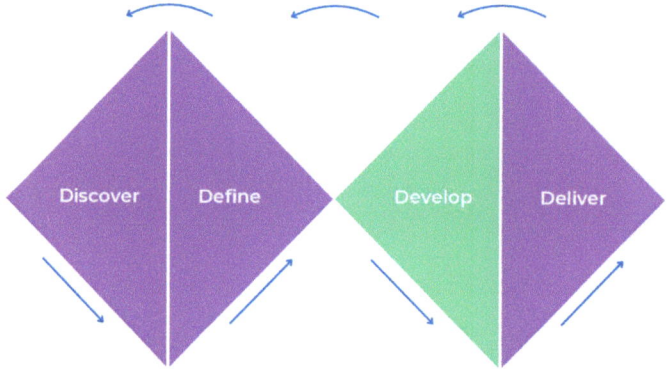

Develop

Develop, ideate, create, conceptualize, design

Now, you can finally start generating new ideas based on the understanding you've gained during the first diamond and reactivating the ones you placed in your pool of ideas while doing research. The more ideas you have, the better your chances of discovering the good one. Don't forget to invite the user to join you in the ideation table, or even better, visit the user and prepare a workshop in their natural environment.

Once you feel you have generated plenty of ideas, probable solutions, or opportunities, create a few more. Next, start filtering them through your decision-making process. In this phase, the understanding that you gained during the first diamond will, again, play a crucial role.

In this phase, you should
- generate ideas
- use your gained understanding in ideation and decision making

Tools and methods for achieving this
- user persona
- journey mapping
- service blueprint
- stakeholder mapping
- Lotus Blossom
- affinity diagram
- Six Thinking Hats (De Bono Group)
- mind map
- empathy map
- SCAMPER
- shitty first draft

Service concept

Susan Goldstein (1) defined the service concept as "the customer's and provider's expectation of what a service should be and the customer needs it fulfills. The service concept defines the how and the what of service design, and helps mediate between customer needs and an organization's strategic intent."

---

1. Goldstein, S. M., Johnston, R., Duffy, J., & Rao, J. (2002). The service concept: the missing link in service design research? Journal of Operations Management, 20(2), 121–134.

Demystifying creativity

Some people think creativity is something that only artists are capable of. That is not true. Mahmoud-Jouini et al. (1) discovered that in some organizations, innovation is highly valued when it occurs in technical R&D groups. But if we want innovation, we need to allow it to happen all around. It's important to acknowledge that innovation that takes place outside the R&D hub is just as valuable. How can we enable innovation and creativity?

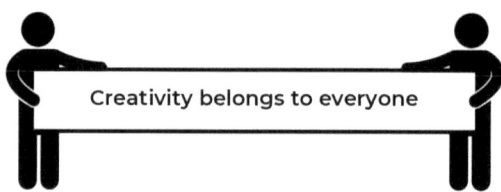

Ingredients for creativity

Creativity may sound fancy, distant, or artistic. This perception of creativity sometimes prevents us from being creative. The truth is, creativity is a teachable skill, and everyone is creative on some level. According to Teresa Amabile (2), personality traits such as independence, self-discipline, orientation toward risk-taking, tolerance for ambiguity, perseverance in the face of frustration, and a relative lack of concern for social approval may help us be creative, but we can also train our creativity through techniques that improve cognitive flexibility and intellectual independence.

An employer or team manager might be wondering how to support the creativity of their team members. According to Amabile, rewards are not the solution:

> "Money doesn't necessarily stop people from being creative,
> but in many situations, it doesn't help" (3)

To build an environment in which creativity can flourish, you should consider the following aspects (2):

- intrinsic motivation
- psychological safety
- freedom
- expertise
- creative thinking/process skills

1. Mahmoud-Jouini, S. B., Fixson, S. K., & Boulet, D. (2019). Making design thinking work: Adapting an innovation approach to fit a large technology-driven firm. Research Technology Management, 62(5), 50–58.
2. Amabile, T. M. (1997). Motivating creativity in organizations: On doing what you love and loving what you do. California Management Review, 40(1), 39–58.
3. Amabile, T. M. (1998). How to Kill Creativity. Harvard Business Review.

You can exercise your mind and creativity

An apt metaphor describes the human mind as an untouched snowy hill with thoughts forming skier paths on top. It's easy for the brain to always follow the same path as it requires less energy than creating a new one. The thing is, if you use the same paths repeatedly, they get too deep for you to see the hill anymore. On some occasions, you can find solutions on the path, but on others, they might be elsewhere on the hill, and you need to get yourself out of your deep path for a wider view. It's fascinating to think that there is always a solution – sometimes we're just in too deep to see our surroundings.

It has been discovered that the thinking paths of Nobel Prize winners have something in common in the face of complex problems. In a complex situation, these people stop working on the problem and start working on themselves and their thinking.

This page summarizes the video "Ajattelun urautuminen" ('Thinking in a rut') by Asta Raami and Helena Åhman (available on YouTube, 2024).

Techniques for training your creativity

The "Yes, and…" technique prohibits the criticizing of ideas. Instead of shooting down an idea you think is not that great, you collaborate by responding 'yes, and…' and build on top of others' ideas.

Think outside your industry.
Can we copy ideas from other industries and modify them to fit our needs? Can we find inspiration in beauty salon products or services in the tourism or construction industries? See, for example, the Experience Pyramid that Tarssanen and Kylänen (1) developed for producing experiences in tourism; could it work in experience design for a pregnancy test?

Mix old and new.
Ideas do not need to be novel to be good.

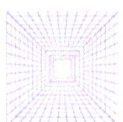

Change perspective:
What would a friend do?
What would the Prime Minister do?
What would Batman do?

Try thinking both in silence and out loud.

Visualize.
Maps and blueprints are not only for design, development and communication purposes. They also serve as tools for ideation.

1. Tarssanen, S., & Kylänen, M. 2006. A theoretical model for producing experiences – a touristic perspective. In: Mika Kylänen (ed.). Articles on Experiences 2 (3rd edition), pp. 134–154. University of Lapland Press.

Holy moly, I need to run a workshop

A workshop is a meeting where a group of people tries to create ideas, concepts, or solutions to a defined problem statement. A workshop needs a facilitator for time management, to enable everyone's participation, and to encourage participants to think big. The facilitator can stay neutral or contribute to the ideation. To run an effective workshop, you must prepare certain things beforehand.

Workshop checklist:

1. Invite the relevant people.
2. Know your participants and consider their needs and strengths.
3. Define your role or approach: **ideating, mentoring, facilitating, teaching,** or **coaching**?
4. Plan the start of the workshop (icebreakers, introductions).
5. Define the topic and goal before ideation.
6. Choose the appropriate tools.
7. Present background information (without influencing the ideation too much).
8. Mute your inner critic. There are no bad ideas at this stage. Encourage the participants to build on others' ideas.
9. Quantity leads to quality. It's more likely a good idea is found among a hundred ideas than ten.
10. Reserve enough time for breaks. (It may be good to sleep on an idea.)
11. Consider the environment (fresh air, light, view, seating).
12. Ensure psychological safety.
13. Consider information and data storage and documentation after the workshop.

There will also be plenty of things you can't plan for. Handling the participants' emotions and group dynamics as well as managing time, focus, and effectivity come with practice. The participants' personal connection to ideas may create conflicts or tension, and it can be useful to stop and talk about the emotions that arise and revisit the objectives of the workshop and project.

Running effective, fun and meaningful workshops is a skill you can learn. There is an abundance of content available about **workshops, icebreakers, energizers,** and **facilitation techniques** for online and offline environments.

Prompt:

- Could you describe the difference between mentoring, facilitating, teaching, and coaching, please?
- Please, give examples of facilitation and coaching methods.

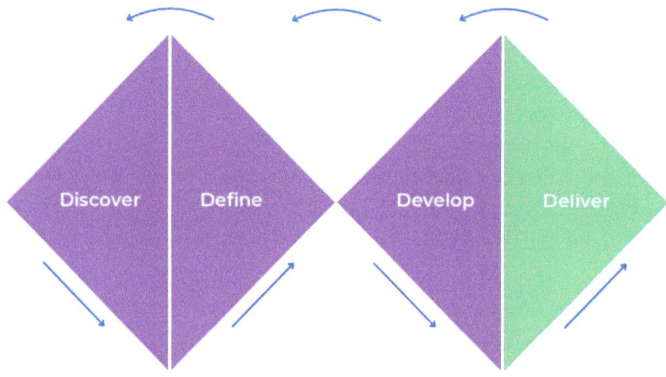

Deliver

Deliver, explain, evaluate, implement

You have now generated plenty of ideas for your specific problem statement. Some of these ideas are most likely either irrelevant or impossible to execute for one reason or another. It's time to test the ideas and concepts and iterate towards the final solution.

Testing and prototyping are crucial parts of the service design process; only by involving the users, can we prioritize ideas and decide which ones to focus on and which ones to discard. When developing a medical device, quick and early testing is essential as development may be resource intensive. The co-creators of this handbook, the interviewed medical device product managers, stated that prototyping is often slow or that they should be doing it more.

Instead of burning money polishing the first prototype for months, we could adopt the culture of quick prototyping, agile collaboration, and dialogue with the user. As Tom Kelley and David Kelley from IDEO (authors of the book Creative Confidence) described (1):

> "There is prototyping that you will showcase to the boss or investors
> and there is prototyping that is done for you (because you don't know the answer!)
> and the team to further iterate."

Another reminder from Tom and David Kelley is that we don't always need to prototype the whole thing. We can also prototype the "unbelievable part", the part of the reinvented version that can be difficult to imagine. The next chapter describes different ways of prototyping.

In this phase, you should
- test ideas or concepts
- iterate towards the final solution
- implement the finished product

Tools and methods for achieving this
- journey mapping
- service blueprint
- How Now Wow
- SWOT
- storyboard
- prototype

Deliver

1. IDEO. Medtech Prototyping. Available on YouTube. Accessed in November 2024.

Prototyping

Prototyping, drafting, and testing can be used in several parts of the service design process for different purposes. Prototyping is an important task for
- reducing risks
- finding out if a concept is technically feasible and fit for its intended use
- validating our interpretation of customer demand
- exploration
- understanding, evaluating, or communicating user behavior scenarios in an inexpensive way.

Essential considerations when prototyping
- Define the purpose of prototyping.
- Set prototyping questions: What feedback do you need at this stage? Who should you ask?
- Provide the feedback giver with enough information about the background and future steps of the project. Tell them if they're dealing with a **looks-like prototype** or a **works-like prototype**. (1)
- Avoid influencing opinions or the testing experience.
- Choose the most appropriate way to analyze, organize, and visualize data.

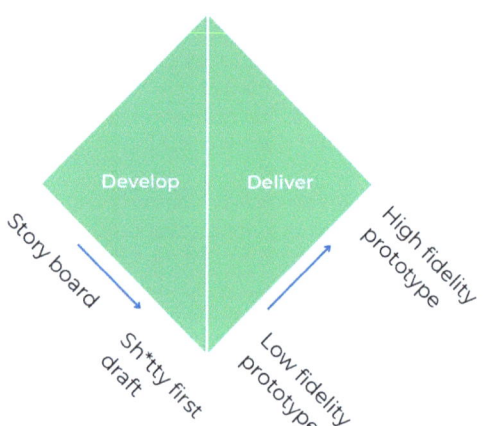

Start with a value prototype

Stickdorn et al. remind, "You can spend a lot of effort and money creating a great look and feel, but if you don't build it on top of a solid value proposition that is backed by research or prototyping, you are very likely to burn money." (1)

A rudimentary prototype assists in communication

Tim Brown emphasizes the importance of quick prototyping as a means of communication. "Prototyping doesn't have to be complex and expensive. In one health care project, IDEO helped a group of surgeons develop a new device for sinus surgery. As the surgeons described the ideal physical characteristics of the instrument, one of the designers grabbed a whiteboard marker, a film canister, and a clothespin and taped them together. "Do you mean like this?" he asked. With his rudimentary prototype in hand, the surgeons were able to be much more precise about what the ultimate design should accomplish." (2)

Tools and methods vary depending on whether you are prototyping a physical product, software, service, or experience.

TIP! Here's a list of different types of prototypes:

- cardboard prototype
- functional prototype
- mock-up
- UI screenshot
- form prototype
- click dummy
- wireframe
- video story

- storyboard
- roleplay
- LEGO model
- process simulation
- template (e.g. Business Model Canvas, service blueprint)
- 3D printing

What's the level of fidelity needed at this stage? How much effort and resources do you want to put into prototyping? Notice that the level of fidelity may impact the quality of the feedback you get.

Low fidelity   **High fidelity**

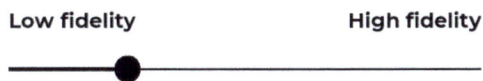

Example: Prioritization based on prototyping
Case: Medical device calibration procedure

X-axis
The user evaluated the use of four different feature prototypes based on how well they solved their problem related to a system calibration procedure.

Y-axis
R&D evaluated the four features based on ease of technical execution.

Ball size
Product management evaluated the commercial impact (e.g. impact on market expansion, branding, advertisement, return on investment, alignment with product strategy etc.) of the four features.

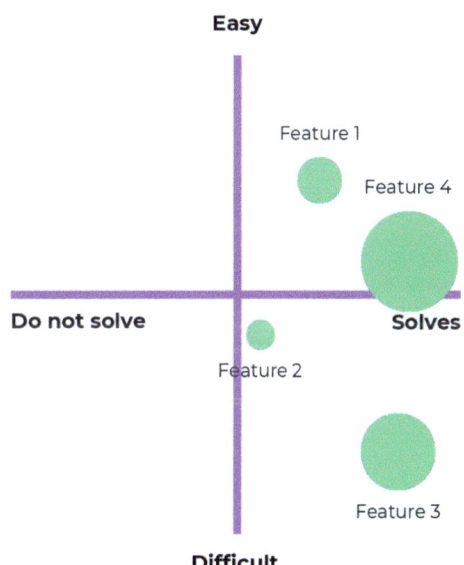

Prototyping medical devices

Many medical devices have users or stakeholders on multiple levels, which complicates product development and prototyping. Stakeholder mapping and journey mapping of different scenarios and users can help understand the complex, multilevel group of medical device users. It's important to define whose feedback you need. For some product types, for example, a family member might be a more frequent user than the patient themselves. Still, both voices must be heard.

Some companies hire nurses, physicians, or laboratory personnel to bring in user understanding. It's a great way to add to intellectual capital and do low-fidelity prototyping but will never fully substitute for prototyping with real users.

After receiving feedback, you might want to express your gratitude or even compensate for the time and effort the user invested in your prototyping activities. However, be careful with compensation and make sure there is no risk of bribery. Often, the users are not seeking compensation but are intrinsically motivated to help develop an improved product they could access in the future.

Excuses or attitudes
Prototyping can be challenging due to attitudes inside the manufacturing organization. These are some of the attitudes I came across during the writing of this handbook:

"I can't make an early quick prototype because..."
- ...I don't want to create expectations by telling the sales team or the customer about the product as it won't be available for another 1–2 years.
- ...it may commence a time-intensive ethical approval process.
- ...prototyping is time-consuming.
- ...it's too early to test with users.

Hopefully this chapter has given you some tools to cope with these types of attitudes towards early prototyping. In an ideal case, prototyping is beneficial to both the user and the manufacturer and saves time and money. Communicating the purpose of the prototype is essential. The information and insights generated through prototyping help implement the final product.

1. Stickdorn, M., Lawrence, A., Hormess, M. E., & Schneider, J. (2018). This is Service Design Doing: Applying Service Design Thinking in the Real World – A Practitioners' Handbook (first edition). O'Reilly.
2. Brown, T. (2008). Design Thinking. Harvard Business Review.
3. Businessdesign.org

Implementation

Service design is not just about research and ideating; eventually, all the knowledge gained through the design process results in the implementation of the final product.

The information and understanding you have gained should also help you decide when the product is good enough. It's a big decision that takes courage. Let's co-create a checklist to define when your product is finished.

Implementation checklist

Your new product or product change*...

☐ ...is compliant with the regulatory requirements and standards.

☐ ...solves your customers' problem.

☐ ...matches your customers' needs and cultural context.

☐ ...is profitable and aligned with the organization's strategy.

☐ What else? _____

---

*) A **product change** in medical devices refers to a change that impacts product performance, safety or intended use, or a smaller change such as a supplier change or documentation update. The change activities depend on the significance of the change. An improved version of a product does not necessarily require a new CE certification process (in the EU) or 510(k) clearance (in the US). Instead, manufacturers can often use a product change control process to evaluate, document, and approve changes while ensuring the product's safety, performance, and compliance with regulatory standards. Regardless of the change control path taken, implementing product changes is resource-intensive and often considered an undesirable situation for manufacturers.

The manufacturer's responsibility doesn't end when the medical device is delivered to the customer. Standards and regulations require post-market surveillance, and in many cases, it's a task for the product manager – or at the very least, their contribution is needed. Next, let's co-create a post-market surveillance journey!

Post-market surveillance

The main purpose of post-market surveillance is to ensure that the device we left with the customer stays functional and safe for its users. The analysis the manufacturer is required to conduct on customer feedback, comparable devices, or advances in scientific research also helps define opportunities to improve the medical device.

The following visualization presents a timeline of possible tasks and required collaboration related to post-market surveillance. When creating your own PMS task list, consider the post-market surveillance requirements relevant to your device risk class and local regulations. You may also want to create separate categories for different stakeholders or tasks (e.g. incidents and scientific advances).

Remember to define and document
- information sources (e.g. literature sources, databases, and registers)
- data collection methods
- methods for analyzing the gathered data
- suitable indicators and threshold values

"My post-market surveillance tasks"

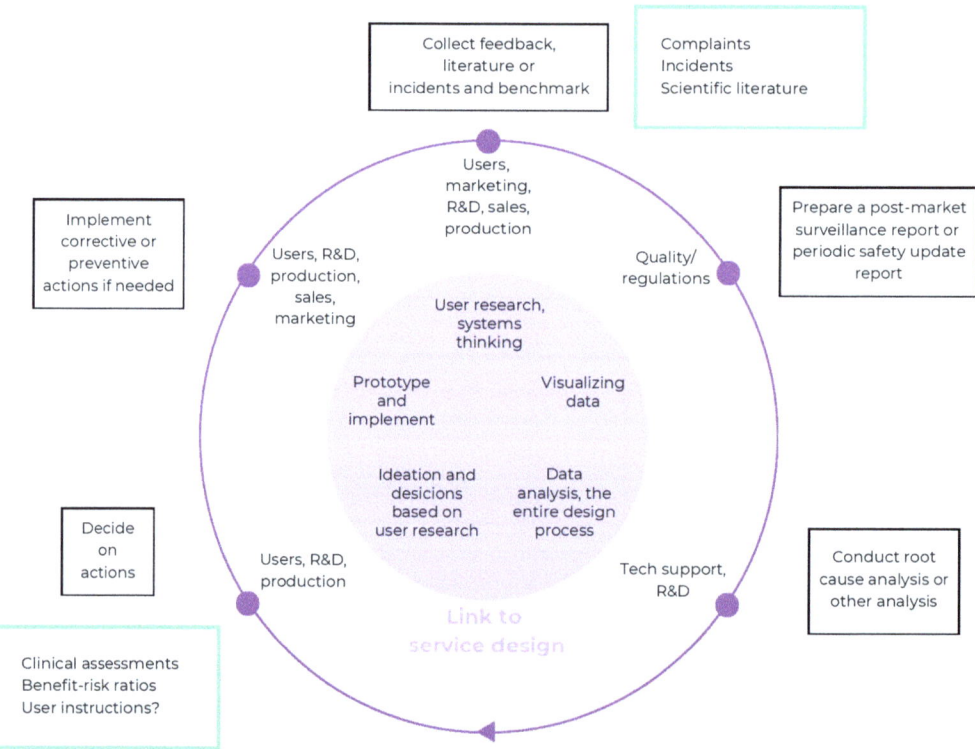

Conclusion

Conclusion & discussion

Standards and regulations emphasize the importance of user-centered medical device product development but do not provide any practical tools. Service design is a systematic and practical approach for improving user involvement in medical device development and assisting product management. Today, products are not just goods; manufacturers need to embrace the service and experience aspect of the product or offering to win over customers who are highly aware of their value and power. In that challenging task, empathy is necessary. Sometimes what we humans (customers, colleagues, you, me) say is different from what we actually do, and observing behaviors can be a game changer.

Service design enables
- deep user research and needs-driven processes, products, or services
- methodological empathizing with the customer
- delivering and (visually) communicating rich and valid user insights to the team
- designing the service/experience aspect of the medical device product
- holistic and/or systemic considerations in product development and management
- effective and purposeful prototyping towards a desirable, feasible and viable offering

Co-creation
Service design is "designing with the customer, not for the customer" (1). In an ideal case, the customer or user is involved in the development process as much as possible. Incorporating different levels of prototyping in the development increases the likelihood of solving the customer's problem and efficient project execution. Iterations or design sprints are not a novelty in medical device development. When done in collaboration with the customer, they increase the chance of discovering opportunities and mitigating risks.

The process and its adoption
The world is not black and white, and neither is the service design process. It's flexible and should adapt to the project, not the other way around. The more you practice, the better you can harness its full potential. Service design can only be learned by doing. While individual product managers can get a lot of benefit out of the service design approach, a joint effort with the organization's decision-makers to adopt service design in the company is essential when **turning talk about human-centricity into action.**

Next steps
After reading this book, you have plenty of basic knowledge about service design, which enables you to start applying the service design mindset, process, and toolbox to your own projects. You don't need to be a service designer to be human-centered, so be brave and start somewhere. If you have a chance to work along a service designer, make the most of it. Once you start using the service design approach, you will experience many eureka moments regarding its adaptability, flexibility, and efficiency. Those moments are impossible to convey through text – they need to be experienced in practice. What's the first step you're going to take to turn words to actions? **Good luck with your future projects!**

1. Stickdorn, M., Lawrence, A., Hormess, M. E., & Schneider, J. (2018). This is Service Design Doing: Applying Service Design Thinking in the Real World – A Practitioners' Handbook (first edition). O'Reilly.

The elevator pitch on service design

in the world of medical devices

An elevator pitch is a brief introduction to a topic. This is an example of how to explain service design to a colleague in the course of a 40-second elevator ride.

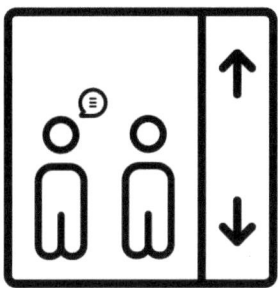

The elevator pitch
Service design is a holistic, analytical and systematic method for designing intangible things such as services, experiences, or business strategy. It's a process, a toolbox, and a mindset. Service design is a needs-driven approach rather than a technology- or product-driven approach.

In medical device development, service design offers practical assistance with empathizing and co-creating with the customer.

In practice, service design employs techniques, tools, and a mindset for understanding users to solve the correct problem. User research, co-creation, and prototyping ensure that the problem is solved correctly.

Service design is an outside-in approach. It's an enhancer of customer experience and organizational performance. (1)

1. Andreassen, T. W., Kristensson, P., Lervik-Olsen, L., Parasuraman, A., McColl-Kennedy, J. R., Edvardsson, B., & Colurcio, M. (2016). Linking service design to value creation and service research. International Journal of Service Industry Management, 27(1), 21–29.

A letter from the future

5 years ago...

Having reached this point in the handbook, you have acquired a lot of information to process. How do you feel now? You are the co-creator of your own reading experience, so I'm asking you to write the last chapter. **You can utilize this exercise in your workshops, too.**

Task: Write an appreciation letter from [your name] written 5 years from now.

For example:

I'm delighted that five years ago I initiated the use of service design in product management. Today, many of my colleagues are aware of service design.

Thank you for being patient and accepting the skepticism of people towards a new approach.

I appreciate that five years ago I slowed down and gave myself time to think and learn.

Further reading on service design

These books include a few pages on medical devices:

- Umar Zakir Abdul Hamid, Suoheimo, M., & Ohio Library and Information Network. (2023). Service design for emerging technologies product development: Bridging the interdisciplinary knowledge gap. Springer.
- Ku, B., & Lupton, E. (2022). Health design thinking: Creating products and services for better health (Second edition.). The MIT Press.
- Pakarinen, A., Lemström, T., Rainio, E., Siirala, E., Pakarinen, A., Lemström, T., . . . Siirala, E. (2023). Design thinking in healthcare: From problem to innovative solutions. Springer.

These books are related to service design in healthcare:

- Jones, P. H. (2013). Design for Care: Innovating Healthcare Experience. Rosenfeld Media.
- Pfannstiel, M. A., & Rasche, C. (2019). Service Design and Service Thinking in Healthcare and Hospital Management: Theory, Concepts, Practice. Springer.
- Pfannstiel, M. A., Brehmer, N., & Rasche, C. (2022). Service Design Practices for Healthcare Innovation: Paradigms, Principles, Prospects. Springer.

TIP!
There are also several interesting podcasts and social media groups related to design thinking and service design that could be of interest to you. Explore what's available in your preferred language!

Acknowledgments

Thank you for reading!

I'm grateful for the time you invested in reading this book and in discovering if it has something new to offer to you. I hope that it will spark further conversations on user involvement and service design in the world of medical devices. I would be delighted if the handbook inspired new case studies and service design success stories on medical devices.

I want to thank all the medical device product managers who participated by answering interview questions, sharing their ideas and expertise during the entire writing process, and reading the prototypes. Without you, this book would not have been the same.

Thank you, Antti Brunni, for co-authoring this book with me. I'm grateful for the inspiring insights on design and the digital perspective on medical devices you provided for our readers.

I thank Riina Iloranta for supervising the master's thesis work behind this guidebook. I admire your gentle but firm way of giving constructive feedback and pushing me forward.

Thank you, prof. Mari Suoheimo, for providing feedback, support, and advice already in the early phases of the writing process. Your book Service Design for Emerging Technologies Product Development (1) has inspired me in various ways during the writing process.

Ilkka Juuso – without your unique article (2), my thesis and this handbook would have looked very different. Thank you for the inspiring discussions and for empowering me to share my bold vision to improve user involvement in medical device manufacturing and to strengthen the union of service design and medical device standards and regulations.

Thank you, Xavier De La Huerta, for creating the cover, visuals, and layout for the handbook, and thanks for all the conversations about design, strategy, archetypes, branding, and whatnot! I appreciate your strong support at home and elsewhere throughout the whole writing process.

And finally, thank you, Lotta Leppälä, for improving the reading experience and polishing the text with your professional and empathetic touch. What a delight to work with you!

1. Hamid, U. Z. A., & Suoheimo, M. (eds.) (2023). Service Design for Emerging Technologies Product Development: Bridging the Interdisciplinary Knowledge Gap. Springer.
2. Juuso, I. & Seppänen, T. (2023). How the service design approach can empower medical device development to reach its user-centered goals. In: Umar Zakir Abdul Hamid, & Mari Suoheimo (eds.). Service Design for Emerging Technologies Product Development: Bridging the Interdisciplinary Knowledge Gap, pp. 101–115. Springer.

Key concepts

Medical devices

According to European Medical Devices Regulation (EU) 2017/745 (MDR) 'medical device' means any instrument, apparatus, appliance, software, implant, reagent, material or other article intended by the manufacturer to be used, alone or in combination, for human beings for one or more of the certain specific medical purposes. (1)

In vitro diagnostic medical device (IVD MD), according to In Vitro Diagnostic Medical Devices Regulation (EU) 2017/746 (IVDR) means any medical device that is a reagent, reagent product, calibrator, control material, kit, instrument, apparatus, piece of equipment, software or system, whether used alone or in combination, intended by the manufacturer to be used in vitro for the examination of specimens, including blood and tissue donations, derived from the human body. (2)

Medical devices and IVD products form a group of very heterogeneous products. In Europe, a CE mark is placed on a product as a sign of an MD or IVD product that complies with regulatory requirements. The products are classified based on risk and intended use, further defining the regulatory requirements. In the US, the FDA (Food and Drug Administration) uses a similar risk-based classification. Additionally, the approval route differs, for example, if the product is new (De Novo) or if the device may help people with rare diseases or conditions (Humanitarian Device Exemption (HDE)), to give a couple of examples (3). MDR, IVDR and FDA address home healthcare devices and professional devices separately through different requirements.

ISO 13485:2016 (International Organization for Standardization) specifies requirements for a quality management system where an organization needs to demonstrate its ability to provide medical devices and related services that consistently meet customer and applicable regulatory requirements. Such organizations can be involved in one or more stages of the life cycle, including design and development, production, storage and distribution, installation, or servicing of a medical device, and design and development or provision of associated activities. (4)

Medical Device Manufacturer

In this book, medical device manufacturer refers to an organization that does research, development, manufacturing, sales, and marketing of medical devices or IVD medical device products.

1. Regulation (EU) 2017/745 (MDR).
2. Regulation 2017/746 (IVDR).
3. FDA, Food and Drug Administration 2024. Available at https://www.fda.gov/medical-devices
4. ISO 13485:2016. Medical devices – Quality management systems – Requirements for regulatory purposes.

Medical Device Product Management

The role of product management can vary greatly from one company to the next. The tasks and responsibilities depend on the type of product or product portfolio that the company provides. Sometimes the title of product manager is used for a person who does sales, while on other occasions, a product manager might spend their time writing technical documentation or designing labels and packages.

The following description is based on interviews of eight experienced IVD medical device product managers in Finland. Medical device product managers often follow the product life cycle thinking that derives from medical device standards and regulations.

What the work of a medical device product manager looks like depends on several factors. The company's size and the product's complexity greatly affect the product manager's responsibilities. One product manager may take care of the entire product portfolio(s), while elsewhere, multiple product managers may handle one complex product (line) together. The tasks vary hugely depending on the product's maturity and the life cycle phase. Sometimes, the tasks are categorized into upstream and downstream product management, downstream meaning the tasks more closely related to product development, and upstream meaning the launch, marketing, and other activities connected to a finished commercial product. The manager of the product manager and their personality, vision, and experience may also have a big impact. Even within one company, the duties may change if the manager changes.

In a medical device company, the product manager serves as a crucial internal link that connects various departments such as R&D, sales, marketing, customer support, field service, production, procurement, quality, and regulatory. The role demands excellent communication skills and empathy. The product manager has the demanding job of aligning all the diverse departments toward a common goal. In interviews, the product manager was described as a 'lonely rider' within the organization or 'the little CEO of the product' who manages the current business and plans for the future.

Standards and regulations play a pivotal role in governing the work of a medical device product manager. While they are crucial and necessary in medical device product development, they can be seen as a hurdle when it comes to product change, for example. The stringent regulations often make product changes expensive and slow, with a minimum timeline of 6 months that often extends to a year or more.

The voice of the customer and user involvement are important parts of medical device product development and often the product manager's responsibility. Unfortunately, organization structure often leads to a situation where the account manager (sales), field service representative, or distributor representative is the one in closest contact with the customer. The customer's voice often reaches the product manager through others.

The interviews revealed a desire and need to improve the product manager's tools and capabilities with respect to user involvement in product development. They showed that patient and user safety is the most important pain, challenge, and responsibility of the medical device product manager. They are in charge of delivering and translating the customer needs to the company throughout the product life cycle from the beginning of the development all the way to post-market surveillance. Elicitation of user requirements and prioritization of features were named as the most demanding tasks of the product manager. An international environment and cultural differences bring certain challenges, and it's impossible to please everyone. The key task of the product manager is to find the essence in the middle of a lot of noise and eventually communicate that internally and externally.

Based on the interviews, product manager onboarding is often a short process, and there is room for improvement in clarifying responsibilities. The interviews also suggested that tasks and duties that "don't belong to anyone" are often pointed to product management. A deep understanding of the different functions of the organization as well as those of the external stakeholders aids the work of a product manager. A medical device product manager's scholarly background in natural sciences or engineering is prioritized over a business background, even though many tasks require a business mindset and skills.

Medical device manufacturers aim to make the customer's life as easy as possible. The less intervention is needed and the more invisible the manufacturer is to the customer, the better. However, due to requirements set by regulations and standards, manufacturers need to communicate with the customer. On top of hard skills in natural sciences and business, soft social skills are crucial for maintaining good relationships.

The product manager could be a natural link to introduce service design in the organization. They have a lot of potential for being the ambassador or enabler of service design in a medical device manufacturing company.

Index